POSITIVE DISCIPLINE

Simple Steps to Encourage Appropriate
Behavior in Children

RANDA LEE ROBERTS

Library of Congress Control Number:
ISBN: 978-0-9842064-2-1

Softcover 1st Edition

This book was printed in the United States of America.

To order additional copies of this book, contact: surfingturtlebooks@gmail.com or by visiting: www.randaleeroberts.com

Send questions to: surfingturtlebooks@gmail.com
Website: www.randaleeroberts.com

DEDICATION

This book is dedicated to my two sons, Shelby and Sawyer, who are my greatest blessings in life and my reason for striving to be the best person that I can be at all times. As your mother I grew in ways that I couldn't have imagined. Being your mother, I learned how to love, trust and support unconditionally, and how to help others through guidance and providing encouragement to individuals seeking to find themselves and their own way.

To all of the wonderful children whose lives I was able to touch, teach, and inspire as an educator who in return inspired me to embrace every opportunity to give it my all, I want to thank you for the honor of teaching you and learning from you.

To my amazing parents, who were both young and inexperienced but who taught me what being a family truly meant through the constant love, devotion, and never-wavering attempts to better themselves in an effort to provide only the best for me and my siblings.

It is because of all of these people and the beautiful smiles, sweet hugs, undeniable love and support that have made my life the most wonderful and fulfilling experience a person could ever imagine.

CONTENTS

INTRODUCTION

The Author who brought you *Children Topics from A to Z: A Guide for Tackling Tough Issues* brings this amazing resource on a subject many parents cringe over, **Discipline**. In *Positive Discipline: Simple Steps to Encourage Appropriate Behavior in Children*, you will learn first and foremost the importance of being consistent when it comes to disciplining children. Whether a single parent, stepparent, married couple, or an individual who works closely with children, you'll discover why parents who lack a plan will also lack the skills to tackle some of parenting's toughest challenges.

As a parent, grandparent, educator, or caregiver of children, there will be times when that little cutie pie will make YOU speak gibberish and want to pull your hair out. But, before you go picking out a wig, you'll be happy to know there is a better solution. This handy reference book, which should be a part of everyone's parenting arsenal, will impress upon you how "keeping one's cool" when times get tough may allow one to effectively maneuver through the many bumps in the road that lay ahead, ultimately leading happily to the other side.

Within the six sections of this book, you'll learn: 1) what discipline is supposed to resemble, 2) how to get children to mind before losing yours, 3) the basics as outlined in Discipline 101, 4) positive strategies to handle specific behaviors, 5) how to manage behavioral challenges that may unfold, and there is a section just for teachers, 6) tips and techniques on handling behavior management in schools.

The comprehensive tips, strategies, and techniques found in this book will help prepare you by supplying you with the facts and effective methods to assist you in raising responsible, happy, well-adjusted children, making everyone's lives more fulfilling and rewarding.

You'll learn tips and the psychology behind:

- Avoiding power struggles,
- Recognizing the significance of gestures,
- How the tone of voice sets the tone of the interaction,
- Establishing age-appropriate expectations,
- Effectively using non-verbal discipline,
- Positive verbal discipline techniques,
- The value of positive reinforcement,
- Implementation consistent consequences,
- Forms of discipline.

You'll also learn effective strategies and methods on how to handle difficult or challenging behaviors such as:

- Aggressive Behavior,
- Hitting and Biting,
- Defiance,
- Disrespectful Behaviors,
- Screaming Toddlers,
- Temper Tantrums,

And so much More!

If you're looking for answers or solutions, or you're trying to establish your own discipline philosophy in order to make parenting simpler, this is the book for you.

OVERVIEW

Welcome to Discipline 101, Defining Effective Discipline. I will be your teacher/mentor in assisting you with discipline that really works. Discipline doesn't necessarily come easy to parents, teachers or caregivers. It is something that we've been exposed to throughout our lives from our parents, teachers, grandparents, and other individuals that have come and gone. We may have some ideas about how we want to do things when we are in a position of authority, but that doesn't necessarily mean that we'll have a clue about how to handle situations that arise. That's why I'm here.

After completing this six-step strategy on *Positive Discipline: Simple Steps to Encourage Appropriate Behavior in Children*, you will have a clear image of your personal beliefs on discipline, the need for discipline, and how you plan to tackle the task at hand.

Part One:
Understanding the Basics

Defining Discipline

Discipline is a form of art. It requires the ability to set limits for your child without preventing him/her the freedom to grow and learn. There are many philosophers promoting his/her ideas on discipline. Truth is, one size doesn't fit all. In fact, effective discipline will have to be determined by the individual or couple who will be teaching and reinforcing it for it to be successful.

There are a few misconceptions on "what" discipline actually is or should be. Typically, discipline is thought, by many, to be about punishment, when in fact it is literally more about teaching right from wrong. There are many definitions of the word "discipline," which you can review by finding it in various dictionaries; however, you'll find that most will reflect something similar to the definition found in Merriam-Webster's Dictionary:

Training that corrects, molds, or perfects the mental faculties or moral character; control gained by enforcing obedience or order; orderly or prescribed conduct or pattern of behavior; a rule or system of rules governing conduct or activity.

Understanding the true meaning of discipline and keeping it in mind whenever a situation presents itself requiring "discipline," you and your spouse should be able to come up with effective disciplinary methods that will teach your child more appropriate and suitable behaviors rather than punishing them for getting something wrong. Effective discipline is an effort to teach your child to learn something from the mistakes that he/she has made in an effort to prevent him/her from making the same mistakes repeatedly.

A Healthy Blend of Parenting Styles:

No two people will ever unite sharing exactly the same ideas on parenting and discipline. In fact, this in an area that most couples will struggle with throughout their lives while parenting children, as no matter how "congealed" they believe their philosophies to be, there will always be something that arises on which the two will disagree. It is important to understand the concepts of Partners in Parenting as without a game plan, children will divide and conquer – it's what they're good at. Couples will want to have a plan in place to help them work through these differences in an effort to prevent disagreements that could potentially lead to marital disharmony.

There are a few things that couples can do BEFORE starting a family which will allow them to identify and share with their partner specific parenting beliefs that they feel strongly about. Through this simple exercise, couples can work together on formulating a parenting plan/style that they are both comfortable with. Of course, if you already have children and you and your spouse are butting heads over discipline issues, you can take these simple steps as well.

- Imagine your child in twenty years. A first step might be for each of you to write down a brief description of the attributes and qualities that you'd like your child to reflect at the age of twenty-five. For example, you'd like your child to demonstrate the use of good manners, to be self-disciplined, and be respectful and kind to others.

Compare your lists to determine the similarities. You now have a starting point.

- Share Parenting/Discipline Philosophies. Review with each other any form of discipline and parenting styles that your parents used when raising you. This is a good time to share methods that you were pleased with and those that you'd rather eliminate from your parenting regime. This might include areas of discipline such as "parenting without yelling" or "washing one's mouth out with soap" for using profanity, etc. Everything is important at this stage because you might find things that one parent may consider acceptable and the other parent not so much. However, you just might be surprised at the number of issues with which you're actually on the same page.

- Establish a plan you can both live with. At this point, you'll need to establish a parenting plan that you both find agreeable. Be specific or it won't be successful. Begin with typical toddler behaviors that you'll experience first, from biting others to temper tantrums, and how you both feel these behaviors should be handled. Continue choosing different inappropriate behaviors, as you'll need to determine what both of you feel is unacceptable or needing modification. There are many disciplinary tools and beliefs for handling behaviors that you both want modified. You and your partner MUST agree so that you can work together presenting a united front. Examples here will be "time out," "loss of privilege" (older children), apologizing, etc...

- Agree to disagree. Situations will occur in which the two of you may not feel that the agreed upon "discipline" is appropriate or necessary. This is when you'll need to have a plan in place to "problem solve" without the children recognizing the dissention. You should have a signal that is used ONLY when you and your spouse need to "take a time out" to momentarily discuss, out of earshot, the situation at hand and come to a common solution.

- Remember, parenting isn't easy. It is one of the most rewarding yet difficult jobs you'll ever have. And no matter how good a parent you and your spouse might be, you are going to blow it from time to time. Giving your spouse the benefit of the doubt will be more beneficial to your relationship as a couple as well as to your parenting esteem. Always remember to compliment your spouse when he/she handles a situation particularly well. It's nice to feel appreciated.

- Know when to ask for professional help. Sometimes couples find themselves divided on issues and cannot find a common ground. It happens, especially in blended families. Seeking the advice of a neutral third party, NOT MOTHERS OR MOTHERS-IN-LAW, can be beneficial in handling disputes. Within your community, or nearby, you will have access to family therapists who are highly skilled facilitators that can often have you and your partner coming together on difficult issues within even one session.

- Visit a library or bookstore. There are thousands of books and videos on parenting that can provide great insight on methods of discipline, parenting styles, and personality traits. Include these resources as tools for your success. Perhaps one of you is more inclined to read than the other. That doesn't mean that you both cannot benefit from the information obtained between the pages. Mark the relevant information within the book, allowing your partner to read just the details that are pertinent. Or, you can read aloud to your partner. Whatever method works to insure that the information is processed.

Remember, as difficult as parenting can be for couples, it is also the single-most important and rewarding experience the two of you will share. Sure, some days you may feel like playing in traffic because your toddler or ten-year old has been particularly difficult, but the good and sad news is that it will pass. Before you know it your toddler will be headed off to college.

You'll look back on the experience and with fond memories, asking yourself, "Where did the time go?"

Believing in YOUR Discipline Plan:

Believing in the plan that you and your spouse have designed to use in raising your family is mandatory, for without your wholehearted belief in the system, it will surely fail. Often parents, especially new ones, cannot imagine that their little "pumpkin" can do anything wrong. It's unimaginable to them how that beautiful, innocent little tot could possibly scribble with crayon on the freshly painted wall, or flush the telephone down the toilet - twice. But, trust me when I tell you that these things and others will happen from time to time, and unless you want to see these behaviors repeated, you will have to do something to modify these behaviors in your child.

Parents must understand that they are first a parent and second a friend or buddy. This is extremely important and something that our generation has allowed to cloud their minds and affect their parenting responsibilities. Without discipline we are doing our children a great disservice. Perhaps we've done it unintentionally, but it has long-term effects that are typically negative in nature.

To avoid falling into this trap, remember the attributes that you and your spouse determined were important for your grown child to possess. Implement the parenting/discipline plan that you agreed upon without hesitation and never allow yourself to fall victim to the following:

- Never feel apologetic for disciplining your child – unless, of course, you've handled the situation inappropriately. It's your job to insure that your child learns from his/her mistakes. Implementing the plan consistently will insure its success and will ultimately reduce the frequency and need for discipline as your child becomes self-disciplined.

- Allowing your emotions to cloud your judgment when disciplining your child can have devastating results. Okay, we all understand that seeing a child experiencing discomfort is difficult to do, BUT it is also necessary from time to time. By going easy on your child so as to prevent him/her any discomfort, you could actually be setting him/her up for a greater level of discomfort in years to come. Remember, it is your job to teach your child how to be self-disciplined. This is accomplished by teaching him/her right from wrong, appropriate vs inappropriate behaviors, and acceptable and unacceptable attitudes and actions. Through your inability to adhere to the agreed-upon discipline plan, your child is likely to grow up without the skill of self-discipline. Without it, your child will likely suffer at school and at work. Typically lacking this skill has a negative impact on their personal relationships too.

- Mean what you say and say it like you mean it. If you sound indecisive through hesitation in your voice and actions when dealing with discipline, your child will "smell it" and use their arsenal to take advantage of you. You must earn their respect and reflect parental credibility, which is equivalent to consistency.

- Some parents go off the deep end and handle matters of discipline like an absolute control freak. Not a good idea if you intend to raise well-adjusted, compassionate, and respectful children. Too much control leads to rebellion in children. It might rear its ugly head in the early adolescent years, but typically it is seen in the teenage years. In cases such as this, parents might want to take a more balanced approach to discipline to prevent the need for more controlling or extreme measures later in life.

When, Why, and How to Discipline:

Knowing when to discipline your child, although to some it might seem second nature, is not always easy. In fact, recognizing when a child has crossed the proverbial line in the sand is often difficult for first-time parents. It is important, however, for parents to begin teaching their children, through modeling of behaviors and role-play, as well as establishing certain expectations of children from an early age. Waiting until the toddler has destroyed the home or terrorized his/her younger sibling is probably too late to begin, although it must begin before it is too late. By making their rules known early in life, parents have a greater opportunity to teach their child right from wrong as each day presents a new challenge. Children will not come into this world knowing the difference between appropriate and inappropriate words, actions, and behaviors. It is up to us to make certain that we teach what is expected.

Having a clear and concise idea of your expectations and how you intend to teach them is necessary. You must also understand how you will implement your discipline techniques in order to insure the desired outcome. Applying your techniques incorrectly can lead to confusion in your child and can ultimately make a situation worse than before. Here are a few tips to clarify when discipline is required, why it must be enforced, and how to properly handle the situation that has presented itself:

- Avoid applying a "one-size-fits-all" disciplinary action. No two children are exactly alike, so why attempt to discipline them as if they are? Discipline must take into account individual children's temperament, likes and dislikes, strengths and weaknesses, and age for it to be successful. Having said this, however, does not mean establishing rules that apply to everyone within the home is an incorrect practice. For example, standardized rules like "keeping your hands to yourself at all times" or "no hitting," "words leaving your mouth must be kind" or "no swearing," "if it goes in your mouth it must be food or beverage" or "no biting," etc., are perfectly reasonable for everyone to follow. However, fine tuning rules as well as consequences will be necessary along the way as you will have to insure that they are appropriate for the individuality of each child.

- It is easy, although unintentional, to find one child the culprit over another. Parents should exercise extreme caution so as not to isolate or alienate the "more often blamed" child. Falling into this trap is particularly easy when you have teary-eyed younger child pointing the finger at the older sibling whom you feel should be more responsible and capable of making better decisions. Often times, you've been played like a fiddle by the younger child. Not only can this lead to extreme resentment by the older child toward the younger child, but it can also result in higher levels of disrespect provided you.

- When anxieties are running high, it can result in parents attacking the child rather than addressing the behavior. Be careful in what you say and how you say it because your child is likely to decipher it differently. A good example of this would be, "I'm so tired of you picking on your sister." Translation, "I don't like you nearly as much as I like your sister." Perhaps relaying your message another way would actually make the point that you intended. For example, "Although I realize your little sister disturbs you when you're , maybe you could respond to her questions using kinder words."

- Positive reinforcement in lieu of punishment is a wonderful method of modifying behaviors and teaching more appropriate ones too. Children's behaviors can be extremely frustrating for parents, especially if the behavior is repeated time and time again. Like, leaving his/her glass on the table after dinner instead of taking it to the sink. Instead of constantly focusing on the negative, recognize and praise the positives. For example, on the occasion that the glass is placed in the sink, make an effort to let him/her know that you've noticed this action and comment on it. Kids will respond much more positively to, "Thank you for putting your glass in the sink," rather than, "Can't you do what you're repeatedly asked to do?"

- Frequently, a parent that does not want to address a particular situation will make excuses for his/her actions, attitudes, etc., "He's sick," or "She just had an argument with her best friend," and the list goes on. Instead of helping your child by explaining away the problems, you're teaching your child that he/she does not have to be accountable for their actions. Bad days happen, so do inappropriate behaviors. Regardless of the reason, children need to be taught accountability and consequence.

- Becoming overly emotional is a "NO NO" as it will result in a loss of credibility in the eyes of your child when and if you must address anger management or related discipline issues. Additionally, through a loss of control you are more likely to make poor discipline decisions. Some children, "bless their hearts," will engage you just to determine if they can create a "melt down." By loss of control, you've just reinforced his/her belief.

- Never give into your child's demands as this is rewarding bad behavior. We've all seen it and perhaps done it ourselves. While in the toy store looking for a gift for another child, your child begins whining about a particular item that he/she would like. Although you've told him/her "NO" repeatedly, he/she repeatedly demands the items. In an effort to reduce your embarrassment as your child has done the ultimate in drawing a crowd, you succumb to his/her demands. Congratulations! You've just created a monster and one that will rear its ugly head and flash its gnarly teeth every time he/she wants something and can manipulate the situation to his/her benefit.

All kidding aside, "No" should mean "No!" and not "I'll think about it," or "Bug me enough and I'll give into your demands." Consider the message that you've just taught your child. (Food for Thought: If you have a teenage daughter who is dating, what word do you always want the boy with whom she's on a date to understand conclusively? NO! Keep this in mind.)

- Probably the most difficult task for parents when it comes to dealing with "out of control" children is to avoid reinforcing bad behavior. If you were lucky enough to get out of the toy store without purchasing the demanded item, congratulations. However, you didn't manage to leave the store without feeling embarrassed, angry, and probably frazzled. Your child has successfully pushed each and every button and probably gotten on your very last nerve in the process, making him/her the winner.

- Avoid making idle threats as this will destroy the effectiveness of even the most well designed discipline plan. Remember, say what you mean and then DO IT! (Unless, of course, you told your child you were going to hog-tie him to the chair if he doesn't stop running around the house.) In other words, kidding aside, tell your child what you expect of him/her and then what you will be doing if the expectation is not met, and do it.

- Although our children will embarrass us repeatedly throughout our lifetime, child development experts stress that we should not embarrass or humiliate our children in return. If your child misbehaves in the presence of others, as a responsible parent, you should quietly take your child aside and address the inappropriate behavior and make it clear that you will handle the issue later and in private. Now, unless this was an idle threat, make certain that you do, in fact, handle the matter and not "forget about it."

Child discipline can be a tough issue but one that all parents must regard as necessary. If you both are clear in your own values and those you want your child to emulate, chances are you will be successful in this feat if you implement a realistic set of discipline standards in your home. Consistency is the key to teaching your children the desired behaviors. Working together with your spouse to present a united front and holding the same set of values and expectations near and dear will assist you in creating a happy, healthy home environment for each of you to thrive.

Part Two:
Making Children Mind without Losing Yours:
Discipline Without Yelling

I hope that you found Part I to be beneficial and perhaps enlightening, and found the tips and suggestions helpful and something that you can incorporate into your parenting arsenal. If you were able to utilize the information shared in Part I, I do hope that you're diving back into the book to experience more tools of the trade.

Prior to moving forward, let me review briefly effective discipline. An effective discipline plan is one that:

- Blends well with your overall disciplinary strategy and child-rearing philosophy.
- Stresses fairness and is reasonable.
- Is suited to your child's developmental stage and individual temperament.
- Focuses on teaching your child to make better decisions and does not focus entirely on punishing the incident of misbehavior.
- Models and promotes respect.
- Is not humiliating, embarrassing, or degrading to your child.
- Is designed to reduce the undesirable behavior and encourage more appropriate behaviors.
- Leaves your child and you feeling good about yourselves.
- Promotes the bond between you and your child.

- Suits both your and your partner's parenting style(s), providing comfort to you both.

I am going to focus on techniques that will encourage your children to listen to and follow your directions or rules without the need for you to raise your voice in order to get them to do so. There is nothing more unsettling to a child (or teenager) than a parent that frequently raises his/her voice when parenting. This, in adult terms, would be like your boss or employer raising his/her voice every time you make a mistake, arrive a minute late to work or are tardy to a meeting, or simply don't do as they demand. Not a good situation for anyone. And one that leaves everyone feeling bad about themselves or the situation.

Parents, we should remind ourselves daily, if necessary, that it is our job to set limits for our children and their job to test those limits, and trust me, they will. This is one "sale" where your child will hold up his/her end of the bargain, guaranteed. Therefore, we must also hold up our end by establishing realistic age-appropriate limits and rules consistently enforcing them and, if necessary, discourage or reduce the frequency of specific inappropriate behaviors from occurring again.

Remember, parenting is not an easy job and is one that sometimes results in our losing control. When we lose control, lots of things can happen. We might say something that we really don't mean, yell, rant, or rave and get off-track, and more importantly, lose credibility as a parent. When this happens, we lose our parenting effectiveness. As parents, teachers, and caregivers, we don't want to make a job that is already difficult ineffective. So, in an effort to eliminate the possibility, let's get started on some "Tools of the Trade of Effective Parenting."

Keep Cool When Parenting:

Children know exactly how to push our buttons. They know what to say or do, how to do it, and when it is the best possible time to rattle our cage to their benefit. It's almost like there is a course available to kids via cartoons that teaches them the skills to get under our skin. This is when WE must exercise good judgment, self-discipline, and self-control with our children. For children, discipline can be like a fishing excursion. They will dangle the bait and wait for us to react and take it. It's the oldest trick in the book and children are masters at it. What is it? It's an invitation to a *power struggle*, and something that will occur throughout their lives and into the teenage years. It is something that we must effectively control in order to avoid the fallout that will occur if we accept the invitation.

Okay, parents, repeat after me, "Say No to a Power Struggle." There are NO winners in a power struggle, unless you consider your child the winner by virtue of the fact that he/she managed to make you lose control. Avoiding power struggles can be simple IF you follow the steps below:

1. **Remain Calm and Avoid Becoming Defiant.** The most important thing that you can do is take a deep breath and take a step back, remaining calm, composed, and in control of the situation. Over-reacting to a situation or incident can result in your loss of credibility in an instant. Although it isn't always easy, parents must ALWAYS model appropriate behaviors. We will slip up from time to time, that's human nature, and when we do, an immediate apology will go a long way in restoring your parental effectiveness and child's faith. But, losing control repeatedly will destroy your ability to bounce back through the eyes of your children. Power struggles require two people - you know the saying, "It takes two to tango." Keeping this in mind, explain to the child that you would like to help resolve the conflict but that it will

have to be done in an appropriate manner so as to avoid hurting either his/her feelings or your own. Temporarily remove yourself from the situation by explaining that you will be in the kitchen, bedroom, etc. When they have calmed down, invite them to join you. Do not engage in further conversation at this point. This will only lead to the escalation of your child's inappropriate behavior.

2. **Use Friendly Action.** It is important to remember that no matter how frustrated, angry, or disappointed you may be with your child you must model calmness in an effort to reduce the levels of anxiety in you both. After all, your ultimate goal is to calm the child. If you and the child are in the presence of others, you need to politely remove yourselves to discuss the matter in private. It is important to maintain your personal space as children can become agitated if they feel you're bullying or intimidating them by touching them in any way. Maintain eye contact and speak in a soft voice using a calm tone. It is important to validate the child's need by paraphrasing what the child has described or by what you've derived from his/her attempts at verbalizing his/her feelings. An example of this would be, "I can see that you are angry about and I understand why you might be angry." This lets the child know that you can communicate calmly and that you're listening to what they are telling you without the need to "grandstand" or disrespectful behaviors.

3. **Win-Win Negotiation.** This is a very effective method in resolving conflict. It should occur after you've calmed the child and paraphrased to the child his/her issue. This is best done by avoiding any form of personal attack that could negatively impact your child's self-worth. Remember, his/her behavior does not mean that your child is "bad." It simply means that he/she made a bad choice or behaved inappropriately. I have found both in the classroom and with my own children that once children are calm, they are much better able to communicate

without anger or fear. Sometimes it will require that you provide the child with "chilling time." What this means is that the child will have an opportunity to "pull him/herself together" BEFORE engaging in conversation. You can let the child know that when he/she feels calm enough to discuss the matter you'll be waiting in the living room, kitchen, etc. Or, you can let the child know that you'd like him/her to take a few moments to calm down and that you'll join them, as you want to resolve the conflict. Once everyone has regained their composure, you can address the situation by stating to your child, "I want you to win. How can I win too?" When children understand that BOTH of you can win, they are more willing to work together with you toward a common goal. I always include a hug, kiss, and words of praise and kindness after resolving conflict. It allows everyone to feel good about the outcome and themselves.

4. **Positive Attention.** Remember that providing positive attention in any relationship is more conducive to eliciting respect and compliance. Children need to know that no matter what; you love them and respect their feelings. By providing your child your full attention regularly, just spending quality time together in which they can share with you what's on their mind, without any advice from you, or free from your trying to teach them something, your child will recognize that you're on their side and feel more comfortable sharing and discussing things with you.

Your enjoyment of parenting is paramount to your success as a parent. Avoid falling into the "power struggle" trap, which will ultimately result in feelings of inadequacy on your part.

Verbal Discipline as a Tool for
Teaching and Handling Misbehavior(s):

There are many methods of discipline from which parents and teachers can pull their techniques. And depending upon the situation, some forms may be more effective than others at eliciting the desired behavior or outcome. Verbal discipline tends to be the one with which adults have the most difficulty often because they don't take everything into consideration as it applies to the situation at hand. Verbal discipline in and of itself is the act of *a) stating your behavioral expectations; b) reminding your child of those expectations in an effort to refocus his/her attention; c) following through with appropriate consequences if the child elects to disregard your instructions.* As simple as this may sound, if handled incorrectly it may not lead to the attainment of your desired objective.

Here are a few suggestions when utilizing verbal forms of discipline to attain the desired behavior or goal:

- First and foremost, ***remember that words can hurt,*** so make certain that you choose words that are positive in nature. This means avoid using phrases that might insult the child or embarrass him/her. The message that you are trying to send should avoid any form of name-calling, for as innocent as it may seem, i.e., "lazy pants," "knuckle head," etc., it can lead to feelings of inadequacy or shame. For example, the statement, "Okay, knuckle head, have you finished your homework?" may lead a child to feel as though you don't think he/she is very smart. Always try to phrase things in a positive manner. Instead of, "Be Quiet!" you can use the phrase, "Please use your inside voice."

- *Use a soft and pleasant voice* when asking or telling your child to do something. By raising your voice you've automatically reduced the level of attentiveness your child will provide you. Instead, whisper or use a soft voice and your child will listen attentively. This goes along with "selective listening." Children will listen as long as the spoken word is kind and non-threatening.

- *Be specific about your expectations.* This is something that few parents get right off the bat. An example would be telling a child to "go clean their room," which is no more effective than trying to get money from an ATM when there are no funds available. Your interpretation of a clean room and that of your child is likely to be worlds apart UNLESS you've actually taught your child what "clean" means to you through modeling the behavior. He/she may pick everything up off the floor and toss it into the toy chest or perhaps they'll shove everything under the bed as to them, out of site = CLEAN. By explaining clearly what you expect you are eliminating the potential for an escalation of verbal discipline. A more realistic and effective statement of expectations would be, "Please clean your room, placing your toys on the shelves where they belong; putting your dirty clothes into the hamper; and your shoes in the closet. I will be back in twenty minutes to see that it is done correctly." This explanation clearly defines your expectation so that your child will not "fall short" in meeting it. (NOTE: If you give them a specific time frame, you'll want to set a timer so that you will remember to follow-up and they will understand that they don't have all afternoon to complete the task). When providing instruction(s) to your child, at any age, you'll want to establish eye contact so that you have their undivided attention. Telling him/her what you want them to do from across the room, while they are watching television or engaged in some activity, will prove ineffective most or ALL of the time. Also note that instructions shouldn't be too extensive - consider the ages and capabilities of your children.

- *Be prepared to follow through.* As stated above, in order for verbal instruction and/or discipline to be effective you must follow through. In stating your behavioral expectation and time frame to your child you've indicated that the task requested must be completed and that you intend to check for yourself that it has been. (Remember standards should be realistic and age-appropriate.) If you become side-tracked and fail to follow through, your child will learn that they have a fifty-fifty chance of getting away with NOT following directions. This will ultimately lead to your child learning that he/she really doesn't have to do what you've requested.

- *Provide reminders as necessary.* Obviously, the younger the child the more necessary it will be to redirect their focus as the attention span of a four-year-old is much less than that of a 14-year-old. Children will become distracted just like adults do from time to time. It isn't unrealistic to provide a gentle reminder when you notice your child has wandered off the path. Sometimes it is even necessary to repeat the same instructions that you provided earlier in an effort for the task at hand to be completed. (**NOTE:** *Teaching young children to follow directions may require that you repeat simple instructions hundreds of times before they are able to internalize and apply them.*) This is especially true in the classroom when teaching classroom procedures for turning in homework, preparing their papers and/or backpacks for departure. Never expect that your child will remember instructions that you presented last week or even yesterday. Learning is a lifelong process and will take time.

- *Verbal Prompting.* If you've reminded a child and still he/she has not completed the task that they've been requested, required, and/or told to complete, you may have to issue a verbal prompt. This might include a warning that he/she will lose a privilege, be required to go to bed early, or even assume another responsibility related to the task at hand should he/she fail to complete the task in the next twenty minutes. Again, make certain that the task is age-appropriate and the time provided realistic.

- *Follow through immediately.* If your child fails to complete what is expected of him/her, you must follow through with the consequence that you determine is relevant and appropriate. Avoid falling into the trap of allowing your child another chance so as to avoid discipline. This will only exacerbate the situation and potentially lead to similar scenarios in the days to come where you may be less likely to control your frustration. Remember, we're either training them or they're training us. Which do you prefer?

- *Avoid making promises.* If you make false or empty promises, or threaten consequences that you don't intend to follow through upon, you will be setting you and your children up for failure. "Say what you mean AND mean what you say!" Telling your child that he will have to go to bed at 9:30 p.m. due to his ill-manner that morning and then NOT following through will teach your child that you don't really mean what you say, so why should he/she listen in the first place? Promising that you'll take your child to the ice-cream shop if he/she makes an "A" on his/her spelling test should mean that the day that you receive the test score you take the child to get ice cream. Nothing loses its effectiveness more quickly than failure to follow through.

You will note that by making your expectations clear and presenting them in a pleasant tone while making eye contact, you've avoided the need to elevate your voice. Even if the task(s) required have not been completed, following the steps above will prevent the need for raising your voice. Demeanor is everything when teaching, modeling, training, and "disciplining" your child. If you maintain control, chances are that your child will follow your lead.

However, that is not to say that you won't have children who will challenge your authority.

If you'll remember from Part I of this series, discipline was described as an opportunity to teach your child the difference between right and wrong, appropriate and inappropriate behaviors, and acceptable and unacceptable words, behaviors, and actions. Being able to recognize and handle behavioral situations as they occur and choosing the best method of doing so is also a learned skill. Parents, teachers, and caregivers don't always have to verbally handle situations needing correcting. In fact, often non-verbal discipline is just as effective.

Non-Verbal Discipline Techniques:

Obviously when utilizing non-verbal discipline as your method of correcting inappropriate or unacceptable behaviors, you aren't using your voice at all, thereby eliminating the possibility of raising your voice or yelling at your children. We've all heard the saying, "Actions speak louder than words," and although it has been applied to other areas of self-discipline, it is also relevant when attempting to discourage inappropriate behaviors in children. A perfect and effective example of non-verbal cues might be when your child is mishandling a book and you've taught your child the proper way to handle the pages, etc. As well as having provided gentle reminders in an effort to attain the desired behavior, walking over and gently taking the book away from the child and placing it on the shelf may be all it takes to make the point. There are other effective methods of non-verbal discipline as well. Here are just a few:

- **Selective Ignoring.** Sounds funny, I know, but it is effective most of the time in attaining the desired goal. It's kind of like selective listening, in that you're actually deciding to handle certain bothersome but non-life threatening behaviors like rude noises, silly faces and gestures, and basic goofiness by ignoring them as long as the behavior(s) aren't getting out of control. Basically, all you are doing is pretending NOT to notice the annoying behavior. Obviously you'll want to exercise this option when the behavior(s) isn't disturbing others, such as slurping from a glass in a restaurant or burping out loud in the library. Exercise good judgment. However, by ignoring the behavior that your child is dishing up in an effort to receive your attention, you are making a silent statement to your child, which results in having saved your discipline energy for battles that really matter such as biting, pinching, hitting, etc. Typically when a child isn't told to stop or hasn't been verbally challenged/disciplined by you, he/she has failed at the attention-seeking behavior and will become bored and stop the behavior, moving onto another more appropriate behavior or activity. You are not ignoring the problem, but simply ignoring the attention-seeking behavior. If, however, your child continues with the bothersome behaviors, you may have to intervene. This can still be handled without addressing the specific behavior. Perhaps re-focusing your child's attention would be justified. For example, bringing up a question related to a trip, class assignment, game that they enjoy, etc., may be all it takes to stop the annoying behavior and generate a conversation, which ultimately provides the attention that your child is seeking, just not in the manner he/she is attempting to gain your attention.

- **Physical Cues or Making Eye-Contact.** Correcting or redirecting inappropriate behaviors can be accomplished by using physical cues such as hand gestures to signal the culprit to discontinue whatever behavior he/she is participating in. For instance, a finger to the lips will just as easily indicate that you want a child to "stop talking or making sounds" as interrupting others by stating your request. Holding your hand out in front of you, similar to that of a policeman directing traffic, to signal a child to stop running or to slow down is also effective. Sometimes all you have to do with children is establish eye contact to get the point across to them that they are doing something that is disturbing you and that you want the behavior to stop. This works for both young and older children alike. Additionally, if a child is misbehaving, simply moving near or placing your hand gently upon their shoulder or hand makes a simple, silent statement that most children understand. If, however, these methods are ineffective you can always direct the child to come to you by using the simple "finger curl" of the pointer finger, demonstrating the universal signal for "come here!"

By utilizing these simple steps in modifying your child's behavior, you have avoided the use of your voice and have established your authority and the need for your child to discontinue the behavior.

Not all discipline has to be negative in nature. In fact, some of the most effective forms of discipline revolve around modifying inappropriate behaviors by simply suggesting more appropriate ones. If you've ever thought about it, one of the first words that toddlers learn is "NO." How sad is this reality? Once a child has mastered it they use it for everything. "Jeremy, it's time to put the blocks away." "NO!" "Susan, let's put your doll down for a nap and eat lunch." "NO!" There isn't a parent out there that hasn't experienced this one word of communication between themselves and their toddler. So let's review some examples of more positive forms of discipline and child behavior modification.

Positive Reinforcement / Rewards for Good Behavior:

Being creative in modifying your child's behavior, both positive and negative behaviors, can be challenging; however, it doesn't have to be. By phrasing your expectations differently, children will typically respond in the manner in which you're intending. Here are some examples of positive child behavior modification:

- **Positive reinforcement can be considered the twin sister of selective ignoring.** By using positive reinforcement you are recognizing praise-worthy behaviors. Some children are starved for attention and will seek any form of attention they can from adults responsible for their care. It isn't unusual for a child that has typically behaved appropriately and not received any form of praise or attention to begin "acting out" in an effort to receive some form of attention, as they are well aware of the fact that children who misbehave receive lots of attention. To them anything is better than nothing. Being aware of this type of response from well-behaved children should make parents, teachers, and caregivers more understanding of the needs of children. There are two types of discipline techniques which fall under this category:

1. **Praise.** Recognizing behaviors that are appropriate and offering specific comments to reflect the desired behavior in an effort to encourage it. Parents, children are quick to recognize a fake when they hear it. When providing praise you always want to make certain that you keep it sincere. Within the context of your praise, identify the exact behavior that your child did correctly. Make certain that you include comments regarding how *they* feel about their accomplishments as opposed to how you feel. A great example of praise provided meaningfully is, "I like the way you put your toys in the toy box without having to be asked or reminded." This identifies a specific behavior that you want

to reinforce. "You are really showing that you are responsible for taking care of your toys. You must feel very proud of yourself for a job well done." Through assisting your child in recognizing his/her success, you are building his/her self-esteem. In the classroom, this tool is most effective in correcting misbehavior and reinforcing appropriate behaviors. I used it extensively and had exceptionally well-behaved students who only wanted to please others, and in so doing, pleased themselves. An effort to correct the behavior of a child who wasn't focused on his/her assignment was as simple as making the statement, "I like the way Justin is working hard to complete his spelling so that he can enjoy free time at the end of the day." By virtue of the words of praise coming out of my mouth, even though they weren't directed to the child that was off-task, the child immediately snapped into action to complete his spelling in order to be able to participate in "free time" too. Expressing thanks to those students who've stepped up their behavior encourages more positive behaviors from others.

2. **Rewards.** Everybody knows what a reward is, and at some point in our lives we've received one for doing something good. It might have been a star on the behavior chart, or a trip to the candy store for cleaning our room. Whatever the occasion, we were rewarded for doing something appropriate and desired by others. For some, however, rewards and bribes are often confused. Let me take a moment to clarify. A reward is something that you earn after the fact for a job well done. A bribe, on the other hand, is something you demand while a job is still ongoing. For instance, a child has been told to walk the dog as soon as he gets home from school as he is a member of the family and needs to be responsible for assuming some of the household chores and tasks. Your child counter-offers and states that he will take the dog for a walk if you'll allow him three scoops of ice-cream after dinner instead of two. Whoa! Don't get roped into bribery to get things accomplished.

Rewards don't have to have a monetary value, and if they do, establish a cap on the budget for rewards. Rewards can be something as simple as playing a board game after dinner, or reading two books instead of one before bedtime. Rewards are effective as long as they are relevant to the child receiving the reward. An example of an ineffective reward would be offering to take both children to the football game when only one child enjoys football. Consider your rewards carefully if you intend to use them to modify or reinforce appropriate behaviors.

Finally, in an effort to encourage your children to modify their behavior(s), probably the most important skill that parents, teachers, caregivers, and children are lacking is the skill or ability to listen. What did I say? *We may listen to the words coming out of the mouths of those addressing us, but are we really listening for the content and meaning of those words?* Often, we are so caught up in our own thoughts that we cannot stop thinking long enough to hear what the other person is saying. Case in point: My late husband, who was a hard worker, had a hard time focusing on what he was being asked or told. One day shortly before Halloween and just after my youngest son's birthday, we were offered a kitten FREE of charge. How thoughtful. I told my son that it wouldn't be possible as his dad and I had just discussed adopting additional pets. My husband said "NO" to me on the topic. So, when my son asked if he could have the adorable kitten, I relayed the information regarding our recent conversation with a firm "NO." Like children will do, he decided to call and ask dad himself. Well, dad, who never really focused on the conversation because he was in the middle of something, listened but **DIDN'T** listen, telling my son, "Sure, why not?" I was shocked but nonetheless happy because the kitten was precious. On our way home I called my husband and asked him what had happened to the "absolutely no more mouths to feed" conversation we'd had just the day before. Surprised, he asked me what I was talking about. I told him that he'd just given our son permission to accept the "free" kitten. His response, "I thought he was asking for a pumpkin." Kitten - Pumpkin???

You get the point. Sometimes we interrupt the words being spoken by interjecting our opinions and/or suggestions, thereby eliminating an entire thought from being shared by the person talking. This brings me to the following:

Modeling Listening Skills in order to Get our Children to Listen:

Nobody likes to talk to someone who isn't listening to them, and THIS is a universally agreed upon feeling and fact. Listening skills begin early in life. It is a learned skill typically taught through observation and modeling of those with whom we engage in conversation. Many factors are involved in teaching discipline and gaining the respect that is necessary for our children to follow our instructions. Having identified listening as a key factor in establishing respect, let me share with you the following steps to becoming a better listener.

- The most important or first step in getting your children to listen to you is for you to **become a better listener yourself**. Demonstrating that you are truly listening to your child, through paraphrasing what they've shared or by assisting them with their words, will strengthen the bond between you and your child (and spouse too). Through the practice of paraphrasing, you'll also establish trust, which is paramount to any level of respect. Without respect, discipline will fail.

- **Get on the same level as your child** (unless perhaps your child is 6'-3" and you're only 5'-4" - it might be awkward asking your child to squat). Being eye to eye with your child is especially important for effective communication. This will provide both parties undivided attention, allowing each to feel as though nothing else matters at that moment.

- **Never interrupt your child.** Let them finish what they are trying to say. It is very difficult for some children to verbalize what they are thinking or feeling. By interrupting them, it is quite possible that they will lose their train of thought and never find their way back on track. Conversely, if you are talking, you should insure that your child does not interrupt you. Tackling this task can be quite a challenge. With younger children, having an object such as a spoon, beanbag, or microphone which serves to remind everyone who has the floor is a good idea. If you aren't holding the item, you may not speak. If, however, your child becomes impatient and interjects, calmly remind them, "It's my turn to talk now. Please let me finish." Additionally, while listening to your child talk, you can gather your thoughts so that you respond to his/her statements appropriately, although you MUST actively listen to what he/she is saying. There are two words that every parent should practice when engaging in listening skills with their children: **"I understand."** These two simple but very powerful words alone can dramatically impact both you and your child's listening behaviors.

- **Respond calmly.** When engaged in conversation and listening to your child, it is imperative that you speak in a soft, calm voice. This reflects the serious nature of your conversation without being indicative of feeling upset.

Positive discipline is a teaching tool, which if used properly, can elicit the desired outcome of modifying a child's behavior. However, in order for discipline of any kind to be effective, listening must be achieved on both the parent and child's part. Without effective listening skills, parents and children will fail to connect on the most basic levels. Establishing respect for one another is dependent upon "active listening" and the ability to demonstrate that you've not just listened to the other party but that you understand what they've said.

Parenting without yelling is possible and preferred when teaching your child self-discipline. By practicing the tips and strategies that I've shared, you will be able to establish an environment that focuses on mutual respect for each individual's feelings. By maintaining a positive atmosphere, establishing trust between you and your child, parenting can be a magical and mutually rewarding experience...guaranteed to prevent you from losing your mind.

This concludes Part II of Positive Discipline. Part III of my six-part series will focus on Accountability and Consequences.

Part Three:
Accountability and Consequences

In Part III of Positive Discipline, I will be reviewing the importance of teaching children Accountability and the Consequences that will follow as a result. For many parents this tends to be the most difficult part of disciplining their child, in part because most children will resist any form of discipline, resulting in elevated anxiety levels for all parties involved, which typically leads to parents losing patience and sometimes their composure. I will share my "Tools of the Trade" with you to help reduce any anxiety that you may feel regarding disciplinary procedures that work, as well as how you can eliminate the battle that sometimes ensues.

Thus far in Positive Discipline, I've shared how to design an effective discipline plan that both you and your partner can agree upon to be used with your family (Part I). We've focused on methods to discipline without the need to yell or raise your voice by simple behavior modification techniques being implemented into your daily discipline plan, focusing on teaching your child to listen in order to encourage them to mind without losing yours (Part II). Specifically, I've addressed:

- How to keep your cool when parenting and the importance of doing so at all times.

- Practicing friendly action vs. bullying or intimidation techniques.
- Win-Win negotiation and its effectiveness for both parent and child.
- Positive Attention to promote respect and compliance from your child.
- Using Verbal Discipline as a discipline tool and effective methods to use it.
- Utilizing Non-Verbal Discipline techniques to elicit desired behavior(s).
- Practicing positive reinforcement techniques and providing rewards for good behavior.
- Focusing on listening to your children in order to get them to listen to you.
- Positive discipline as a method of establishing respect for one another.

In Part III, I will be focusing on Accountability and Consequences. Teaching our children accountability is fundamental to a child's growth and development. It is necessary as it affects how they deal with persons of authority, relate to their siblings, and associate with peers. Without these fundamentals, children may transition into adulthood without understanding that they, too, must be accountable for their actions.

Often, people describe or believe that responsibility and accountability are interchangeable. They are not. Personal responsibility is one's ability to take care of oneself by means of keeping healthy, managing one's emotions, keeping a sound mind, treating oneself and others with respect, and the capability to function within society without superior authoritative guidance. Short and simple, it is 'the power or ability to act appropriately.' It is defined as a personal quality, not a burden imposed or qualification conferred from without.

Accountability, on the other hand, **CANNOT** be shared. We often hear the term "shared responsibility," but there is no such thing as "shared accountability." Some would call that term an oxymoron. One could define accountability as the "ultimate responsibility." Perhaps it would help to think of one of the quotes that former President Harry S. Truman said, "The Buck Stops Here." It is probably the clearest and most well-known statement of accountability ever made, and it leaves no doubt in one's mind as to where the ultimate responsibility lies.

Everyday life experiences provide the perfect setting for teaching children accountability and consequence as they relate to the decisions they make. However, children will continue to avoid the responsibilities to which they've been assigned as long as earth rotates, and they'll need to step up and be accountable for their decisions, words, actions, or lack thereof. With accountability comes consequences. Or at least consequences should be enforced in an effort to teach accountability. (For more on teaching children accountability, please review the topic entitled "Teaching Children Accountability," which can be found in my parenting series, *Children Topics from A to Z: A Guide for Tackling Tough Issues*). If you intend to teach your child how to function appropriately in society, you must enforce consequences whenever children lack responsible behaviors and demonstrate inappropriate or unacceptable attitudes and actions.

Let's focus our attention to various forms of discipline that can be used in an effort to teach our children how to be accountable through suffering the consequences for their behavior.

As with personal hygiene, safe driving habits and skills, and responsibility, children must learn what consequences are and why we use them. They must be taught just like each of the areas above.

Teaching Consequences:

There are two types of consequence: Natural and logical.

1. Natural consequences are consequences that result from a child's own actions. For instance, if your child throws his cell phone at the wall in a fit of rage and breaks it, he should go without a cell phone until he is capable of replacing it himself. Additionally, if any damage to the wall results from his poor choice, he should be held accountable and should be responsible for repairing the damage at his expense. Natural consequences can be the most effective way of teaching children how to learn from the mistakes that they make as the end result is clearly linked to the child's actions. Your child will learn from natural consequences that he/she has no one else to blame but himself.

2. Logical consequences are consequences that you (or you and your child collaboratively) come up with in an effort to teach your child an important lesson. Note: Please see the topic on "Joint Problem-Solving" in my parenting series, *Children Topics from A to Z: A Guide for Tackling Tough Issues,* as it mimics how collaborative consequences can be accomplished through working together to establish relevant consequences. Logical consequences can be applied to pretty much ANY situation, whereas natural consequences cannot. Obviously for a child who jumps on the bed after being repeatedly requested, asked, and reminded to stop it would be difficult to allow the application of a natural consequence such as a large gash across his face because he wasn't listening to or following your instructions to discontinue jumping. In this case, a logical consequence is more realistic. For example, making your child sleep on a sleeping bag on the floor vs. allowing him to use his bed which he believes is a trampoline will teach your child that you mean business. Harsh, not really. Effective... definitely! Logical consequence must make sense to the child to be

effective. If your child has broken the window because he was tossing a ball near or inside the house, making him fold laundry offers very little logic in an effort to prevent him from throwing the ball and breaking a window or something else.

When choosing consequences to teach your child a lesson, whatever the lesson you are attempting to teach and/or reinforce, you must make certain that the consequence is relevant such as outlined above. Because, when the crime doesn't fit the punishment, children become confused and cannot connect the dots. After all, remember the purpose of effective discipline is to teach your child, not simply to punish him/her. There is the other extreme, which is not holding children accountable for their actions and allowing them minimal consequence. In order to avoid the pitfalls of both ineffective discipline techniques above we will review additional pitfalls that will result in "teachable moments" going to waste:

- Attempt to expedite the consequence (punishment). If you allow too great a delay between the inappropriate action and behavior, a.k.a. "the crime," before enforcing the consequence, a.k.a. "the sentencing," you will lose the effectiveness and "teachable moment." Unless you are delaying punishment due to your level of anger, which is warranted as you are more likely to make poor discipline decisions, you should exercise a speedy consequence. Additionally, there are times when you are unable to discipline your child due to surroundings which may embarrass your child, therefore resulting in your need to postpone the consequence. Make certain, should this be the case, that you quietly let your child know that he/she will be punished, but that you will deal with the situation in a more private setting, such as upon your return home, in order to provide him/her respect and avoid a situation that may result in humility. REMEMBER TO FOLLOW THROUGH!!!

- Selecting overly lenient consequences. If the consequence is something that your child can live with, again, without blinking an eye, he/she may likely commit the same offence. Children will weigh the cost of punishment against the reward (offence) and decide if the punishment is worth it. Make certain that you utilize the "teachable moment" to make a difference in your child's future decisions with the lesson deterring him/her from a future recurrence of the behavior in question.

- Implementing punishment that is overly strict. This one typically occurs when parents react instead of responding to the offence the child has committed. It is a frequent result of anger leading the way. This type of punishment, categorized as "over the top," is one that makes teaching a lesson less effective than by choosing logical consequences. Parents should remember the ultimate goal of disciplining their children is to teach them to make better choices. If you are incapable of calming yourself in an effort to effectively determine a logical consequence it is all right to express your need to evaluate the situation more clearly in order to make a better discipline decision.

- Choosing humiliating consequences. Child experts agree it is imperative that you avoid discipline techniques that are designed to embarrass, humiliate, or degrade your child, and this doesn't imply that it must be in front of others to create the end result. Children may comply with your ineffective disciplinary efforts at first, but as they grow and mature your tactics will be clearly seen as unfair and cruel by your child. Often this type of discipline can lead to feelings of resentment and typically erodes the bond between parent and child. It is not uncommon for a child that experiences this type of discipline to attempt to "get even" with the parent, resulting in repeated episodes of misbehavior.

- Implementing unenforceable punishments. Choosing discipline that is too difficult to enforce, or is unenforceable, is pretty much ineffective. For example, your teenager uses the family car and fails to put gas in the tank, returning it home with not enough to make it to the gas station on your way to work. Consequently, you run out of gas. Your discipline: you tell your teenager that he may not use the family car for two weeks and that he'll have to walk to martial arts. Problem: you live twelve miles from the facility in which your son has lessons. Bigger Problem: you either punish yourself by becoming responsible for driving him to lessons and waiting until they are completed in order to drive him home; or he misses his lessons for two weeks, which does not make good use of the dollars spent paying for the lessons; your son catches a ride with a buddy, which isn't something you consider safe. This is an unenforceable punishment.

- Choosing punishments that punish everyone. Disciplining your child who is behaving rudely and disrespectfully in the car on your way to the movies with the entire family by turning the car around and heading home is disciplining others who have not been disobedient, disrespectful, or rude. What lesson are you teaching?

- Long-lasting punishment. Sometimes parents react by putting the cart before the horse when it comes to assigning discipline. For example, taking away privileges such as cell phones, computers, gaming systems, AND watching television for an entire month vs. taking away one privilege at a time for less time. Grounding your child until he's 20 may sound like a brilliant idea, but is it effective? Let's find out.

  - If you take EVERYTHING that your child enjoys away at one time, what do you have left should the punishment be ineffective? What you've done is exhaust your "privilege bank" and have no other valuable tool to utilize. By taking away privileges one at a time – and one day at a time instead of a month at a time, you've turned that one-month chunk of time into 30 separate things you can take away.

- Grounding or punishing your child for extended periods of time leads to rebellion, making the consequence counterproductive. Extended consequences often lead to your child feeling hopeless in that he doesn't know if he'll be able to behave long enough to have his privileges reinstated. When a child loses all hope, he/she also loses the incentive to behave. This situation often results in major battles between parent and child.

I've just addressed pitfalls that can easily destroy effective discipline techniques. Teaching children how to learn from their mistakes is more easily accomplished when parents are taught how to determine effective consequences. There are many forms of discipline that parents have used throughout the ages. Many result in the desired modification of behavior(s) in our children, while others are simply ineffective and pointless. Being able to determine what will work best is a key element in teaching our children right from wrong.

Obviously, the most important area to consider in choosing discipline tactics is the age of the child. Discipline must be age appropriate if you have any desire for it to be effective. Additionally, being able to choose discipline and/or consequences that are relevant to the child's likes, dislikes, temperament, and offence must be considered too. Let's review some discipline techniques that can be used at home, grandma's house, or at school.

Forms of Discipline:

Most parents, teachers, and caregivers are familiar with "Time Out" as a form of discipline. But, time out isn't always as easy as it sounds.

Obviously this is a form of discipline that must be age appropriate, as telling your 16-year-old to go sit in the "no no" chair isn't going to go over well.

Additionally, telling your one-year-old to sit in the chair and face the corner without moving, giggling, and/or making a sound is like telling your husband not to snore. It just isn't going to happen without supervision (or a very thick pillow). Time out should probably not begin until a child is 18 months of age and is less effective once a child is seven years old. Using time out is forcing your child to remove him/herself from a particular situation so that he/she can reconsider his/her behavior. For example, if your seven-year-old son is picking on his younger brother at the dinner table by making faces and he is instructed to go to timeout for five to seven minutes, he'll probably return to the table with a new mindset and his energies no longer focused on his younger sibling but on eating the food upon his plate... which is probably cold by now (natural consequence). You've just utilized timeout in an effective disciplinary manner. To make timeout effective, let's talk about things to consider:

Timeout:

- **Understanding Timeout.** A child must understand why he/she is being sent to timeout in order for it to be effective as a form of discipline. They must also be taught how timeout works. Explaining why your child is being placed in timeout and what he/she is to do while in timeout is necessary for it to be meaningful to your child. Simply shouting, "Go to timeout" when your child is banging a spoon on the table isn't going to get the point across nor discourage him/her from repeating this behavior. By explaining to your child that he/she is being sent to timeout because of the inappropriate behavior of banging his/her spoon on the table, your child will first understand his/her offence. You will also need to direct your child to "think about what you should have been doing" – eating your soup, and how you will not repeat this behavior again. You can also identify the hazards associated with the offence. For example, "You could have accidentally hit your bowl with the spoon, causing it to spill on you, and that could burn you." Children need the entire picture painted in order for them to understand. In time, they'll be able to replicate this process without your assistance.

- **Choosing an Effective Timeout Location.** Choosing a location that is "distraction free" is important so that your child can focus on his behavior instead of what his younger sibling is doing in the family room. If your child is young, serving timeout in the same room with you might be necessary in order for you to observe and insure his/her safety. If the child is older, another room in the house (not his/her bedroom) might be considered. Why not his/her bedroom? Timeout should not be served in a child's bedroom as we do not want a child to associate misbehavior with going to his/her room. A child's bedroom is a space that a child should recognize as his/her special place, and associating it with a negative could prevent him/her from having a private place to escape when he/she needs time alone from others. These days, timeout goes by a variety of names such as "naughty spot" or "time-out spot" and even "attitude adjustment area," which is what I referred to timeout as within my classrooms. Today parents can purchase "specialty rugs" that can be placed anywhere and which children are expected to sit upon. This could be a good alternative to a chair, which a child may inadvertently flip over if behaving disobediently.

- **A timer or clock should be utilized.** This is a key element in utilizing timeout. If you don't have a timer or clock that can be used, get one, because if you don't the entire time your child is in timeout he/she will be asking you if their time is up. Just like when traveling – are we there yet? Instead of focusing on their violation, they'll be violating their consequence by communicating with you. Place the timing device where the child can clearly see how much time remains. Additionally, it is always a good idea to have a device with a sounding alarm so that you don't become side tracked, leaving your five-year-old in timeout for twenty minutes.

- **Length of time matters.** Timeout isn't intended to be a life sentence. It is only to provide your child enough time to think about their actions, review their decision to misbehave, and come up with alternatives to their inappropriate behavior. It is suggested that parents utilize one minute of time-out for every year of age. Too much time in timeout can actually be counterproductive.

- **Timeout is your child's problem – not yours.** This can be especially difficult for parents to enforce, but extremely necessary in order to have the desired impact and results. For the child that refuses to serve his/her time-out, a clear statement must be made regarding the fact that everything the child enjoys will not exist until his/her time in timeout is finished. For instance, there will be no access to television, music, conversations with friends that may call, and even participation in practice. With the elimination of all things important to your child, including food and beverage, your child will be more inclined to serve his/her time. Note: As difficult as it might be for parents, hugging or coddling a child who has been sent to timeout is a "no no" as it may encourage your child to repeat the offence in order to get this type of attention. I'll address a more appropriate time for hugs and kisses below.

- **Allowing time to be postponed.** Sometimes we cannot enforce a time-out when the misbehavior occurs, such as in the morning when your child is on his/her way to school. You need to let your child know of the consequence and that immediately upon return from school he/she will serve the required timeout. If you typically provide a snack upon your child's return from school, this too, will need to be postponed until his/her time-out is complete.

- **Silence is golden.** When your child is serving a timeout and he/she insists on talking, yelling, crying, antagonizing a sibling or you, and perhaps kicking the chair, you'll need to maintain your silence and reset the timeout clock. This may go on several times before your child realizes that you aren't playing games and that he'll/she'll have to conform to the rules of timeout.

- **Observation is necessary.** After a child serves timeout it is sometimes necessary to closely monitor his/her actions in order to allow you the opportunity to praise him/her for improved behavior. If, however, the misbehavior continues, you'll probably want to teach your child more appropriate behavior(s) to avoid him/her getting back into trouble for the same offence. When I was teaching and my children were of the age that timeout was appropriate, prior to releasing them from time-out they were required to 1) apologize for their inappropriate behavior; 2) identify the inappropriate behavior or actions; 3) explain to me how they were going to modify this behavior in the future to insure that they wouldn't commit the same offence. This technique reduced nearly 95% of repetitive behavior both at home and in my classroom. Upon releasing a child from time-out, I always provided words of encouragement and a hug to let the child know that even though his/her behavior may have been inappropriate and/or "bad," he/she was not, and I still loved them. Sidebar: I will be addressing "how children should be taught to apologize" in another book.

- **Timeout when away from home.** Children choose some of the worst times to act out, requiring us to enforce timeout. Some children behave inappropriately while you're in the grocery or other type of store; some will wait until you're in the dressing room in the clothing store; and some will challenge you while driving down the highway. They know exactly when to ruffle our feathers, knowing that we're somewhat defenseless. If this happens to you, you'll need to have a plan. For example, suppose you're in a restaurant and your child begins to misbehave, thinking that punishment isn't possible. You need to make it a point to enforce timeout to prevent this type of behavior from occurring again. Ask the waiter if you can utilize an empty table for timeout. I'm sure they'll agree as your child's behavior is likely disturbing other customers and they'd all like it to stop. If, however, you are unable to enforce timeout where you are, explain to your child that it will be served upon arrival at your destination.

- **Overusing timeout.** Over-utilizing timeout results in its ineffectiveness. It should be used sparingly and perhaps for a few specific situations, such as those taking place in the presence of other people. An example of a good time to use a timeout would be when a child is acting out during a playgroup or on the playground. Removing the child from the desired environment where he/she can no longer participate will have a stronger impact than placing a child in timeout for dumping his/her glass of milk on the floor. A natural or logical consequence would probably be more effective in correcting this type of misbehavior.

If you elect to use timeout as a form of discipline you will undoubtedly experience the child who refuses to remain in timeout. In this event, should it continue for an extended period of time, perhaps utilizing another form of discipline would be more suitable. Removal of a privilege, going to bed earlier than usual in an effort to get adequate sleep so that he/she may have a better attitude and make better decisions the following day, etc., would be a form of a logical consequence. Timeout will eventually prove ineffective and you may choose alternatives to timeout. Obviously, there will be children who do not respond positively to time out as a form of discipline. When this occurs, you'll want to have a backup plan established, ready and waiting

Alternatives to Time out:

- **Taking away privileges.** Most parents consider privileges something that a child is allowed to do that otherwise he or she would not. For example, in the case of a teenager, using the family vehicle can be considered a privilege, which makes taking it away an excellent form of discipline, or as a consequence in an effort to teach responsibility and accountability, or in an effort to modify a behavior or eliminate a behavior. For others, a privilege such as the use of a cell phone, television viewing privileges, and/or access to a computer or video games might be viable for obtaining the desired behavioral goal. As with any consequence, the more logical the consequence the more effective it will be in eliciting the desired behavior. Such would be the case of a parent overhearing his/her child using profanity while talking on his/her cell phone to a friend. Obviously this behavior is inappropriate and offensive and should be handled in a manner that will get the point across. A logical consequence would be taking away his/her phone privileges (and phone) for a couple of days in an effort to clean up his/her vocabulary. This is not to say that the punishment MUST relate to the particular crime, but that you will get more bangs for your buck when the punishment fits the crime.

- **Eliminating opportunities for social engagements, a.k.a. "Grounding."** This is typically a better form of discipline and consequence for older children that have opportunities to engage socially with their friends after school and on weekends, although it is effective for preteens as well. Preventing your child from participating in a swim party or going to the movies with friends makes a statement that your child's behavior, attitude, and perhaps grades will have to improve before they will be awarded an opportunity to socialize other than during school hours (which is obviously not the best time and could be the reason for their situation in the first place). This is a great motivator for "getting one's act together" and was used effectively with me in order to motivate me to earn a better mathematics grade when I was in high school. Cruel – it will seem like the end of the world to your teenager that cannot attend the school dance because she didn't make curfew two times in one month. Guess what, she'll think twice about being late again.

- **Spanking as Discipline.** Obviously this is a form of discipline that is very controversial and one that I'm neither suggesting nor denying be used as a disciplinary tool. I'm simply going to address it as I know some families utilize this form of punishment in their homes. A swat on the bottom to obtain the awareness of your child that is running toward the street unaware of the cars passing by or to the hand of a child reaching toward the lighted burner of the stove may be considered an appropriate form of discipline in an effort to prevent injury and keep your child out of harm's way. The ultimate goal of discipline and teaching consequences is to TEACH your child to make better choices, NOT to instill fear. We want children to respect us – NOT be afraid of us. If you choose to use spanking as a form of discipline, let me share a few statistics with you so that you are aware of the ramifications. A) Research suggests that children who are spanked regularly as a form of punishment are less trusting of their parents and feel less of an emotional bond with them; B) The more frequent and/or severe the spanking, the less connected a child tends to feel to others; C) Spanking has been associated with a lowering a child's self-esteem as he/she may begin to see themselves as unworthy; D) Spanking has a tendency to send mixed messages to the child in that parents who spank their children for hitting others are illogical to the child suffering the spanking. They will question why they are being hit for hitting someone else; E) Parents that choose physical force to get their child to do something that is required or desired teach children that aggression is the way to get what they want.

- **Positive Reinforcement and Rewards.** When teaching children right from wrong, appropriate from inappropriate, and acceptable versus unacceptable behaviors, using a positive approach in the form of rewarding the positives instead of always punishing the negatives is an excellent way to encourage desired behaviors. Incentives are very powerful tools when attempting to modify child behaviors. This is true for young children and adults too. Positive vs. a less punitive approach will help your children learn to address their behavior without tearing them down and possibly having a negative impact on their sense of self.

Positive discipline includes everything from establishing rules and expectations for your children to follow and/or meet, emphasizing listening skills on the part of you both as well as that of your child, and choosing consequences that will provide teaching opportunities vs. intimidating your child into submission. Consequences are vital to teaching your child accountability and inducing responsible behaviors. If administered correctly, your child will immediately benefit and begin modifying the behaviors needing to be changed. If, however, your punishment(s) don't provide the learning opportunities that you're hoping will be reflected in your child's future decisions and actions, you may need to re-evaluate the consequences you have in place.

This concludes Part III of Positive Discipline. Next I'll isolate specific types of inappropriate behaviors and identify methods of effectively altering them in a positive manner.

Part Four:
Dealing with Specifics (Behaviors, that is!)

In Part IV, I will focus upon Dealing with Specifics. Children are funny little creatures and do some of the oddest things in order to gain our attention. A lot of parents, teachers, and caregivers exhaust all known remedies and/or solutions for handling certain behavior problems to no avail. They become just as frustrated as the children who are misbehaving. In an effort to prevent the potential explosion that is likely to occur should the adult in charge reach wits' end, let me share more of my "Tools of the Trade" to help you nip the problematic behaviors.

First, however, let's review what we've already covered in Part(s) I, II, and III of Positive Discipline. I've discussed "How to" create an effective discipline plan; we reviewed creative and logical methods of teaching children to listen in an effort to eliminate yelling as a form (ineffective as it may be) of discipline; I've reviewed teaching accountability through the use of imposing both natural and logical consequences to teach children the difference between right and wrong, appropriate and inappropriate, and acceptable and unacceptable behaviors by modifying said behaviors.

As a former classroom teacher I got to see and deal with, on a daily basis, all kinds of disciplinary issues from aggression towards adults and classmates to children blaming imaginary friends for misbehavior(s) they'd committed. For some reason, I had a special knack for handling and teaching children who had and/or demonstrated greater disciplinary issues than my co-teachers, and therefore it always seemed that on the first day of school I walked into a landmine. As the other teachers whispered amongst themselves about my class roster, I welcomed the challenge and knew that in no time I'd have the children walking to my rhythm and more behaved than any teacher's classroom full of students.

Teaching and raising children is more than just teaching children how to behave in accordance with the expectations and standards that you establish. It is about understanding the reasons for their actions and being proactive in order to reduce the frequency and/or eliminate inappropriate behaviors and attitudes BEFORE they arise. Like I said, children are odd little creatures, and just because they say they don't want ice cream doesn't necessarily mean they don't want anything. It could mean that they want a hug instead. Reading the cues (body language) and listening attentively will help you determine what a child really wants and/or needs BEFORE an ugly situation presents itself. But, when dreaded moments occur, it's nice to be prepared by knowing how to handle certain situations in advance.

Let's begin by identifying particularly difficult behaviors and why they frequently occur, and then tackle effective methods in resolving these conflicts and modifying the problematic behaviors into more acceptable ones.

When dealing with specifics, certain childhood behaviors, attitudes, and actions can make even the most level-headed individual want to play in traffic. No matter how much you think you know, it's never enough to handle those little firecrackers whose main purpose in life, it seems, is to make you explode. These same little torturers were once the adorable little infants and perhaps toddlers (if you were lucky) that you couldn't wait to dress and play with once upon a time. Where did the time and innocence go? Luckily, you can recapture the happier moments in time by effectively handling situations as they occur, or better yet, before they happen. Let's talk details, shall we?

Let's review and tackle the top five most difficult and challenging behaviors. I will begin with Aggressive Behavior, as this area is quite problematic and tends to be difficult for parents, teachers, and caregivers alike.

Aggressive Behavior:

- *Aggressive behaviors* come in all kinds of packages - so what is aggression? Aggression is a forceful action or procedure, typically unprovoked, in an effort to dominate and/or control another. Put another way, it is hostile, injurious, and/or destructive behavior or attitude often resulting from frustration.

- *Where does aggression come from?* Children aren't born aggressive, they learn it. It can be attributed to frustrations related to or resulting from cultural and social circumstances. Typically with children, family stresses and both positive and negative interactions of the family influence a child's tendency to behave aggressively. Children will model the behaviors of others that they observe and imitate how they handle anger and frustration(s). Note: Television and movie viewing is also attributed to teaching children aggressive behavior.

- *Contributing factors to aggression:* Aggression has been tied directly to a child's (or individual's) temperament and the coping skills that have been learned and/or reinforced, which are responsible for how he/she manages aggression. Temperament is one part of the personality that has been linked to genetics. There are three identified temperaments: a) flexible or easy (go with the flow mentality), which accounts for approximately 60% of all children; b) the next being described as fearful and sensitive, which can be attributed to 25% of the childhood population; c) and the remaining 15% are considered to be feisty or difficult.

- *Why are children aggressive?* Many children lack the social skills and self-control to manage their behavior. They become frustrated when they are unable to find the right words to express themselves and act out accordingly. They may take their frustrations out on individuals who are not directly related to the problem(s) leading to the frustration in the first place if they happen to be in the wrong place at the wrong time.

- *What does aggression look like?* In infants, typical behaviors associated with aggression are crying and biting. On the contrary, the happy child is demonstrative of cooing and babble. In toddlers, most aggression takes place over toys and should NOT be confused as children learning how to get along. At the preschool level children are less likely to demonstrate aggression as they have learned to communicate their needs. However, if a child has aggressive tendencies, they will appear via hostile interactions with classmates. By the time children enter primary school, and usually between the first and third grades, they are more capable of controlling themselves and their actions. Whereas they may hit a sibling, they aren't likely to strike a friend at school. Aggressive children at this age are more likely to slam doors, stomp their foot, and even yell, and will typically behave in this manner at home. By the fourth grade, children who continue to demonstrate aggressive behaviors will typically continue to behave aggressively into their teenage years, and it will be in the form of direct confrontations and physical attacks in males. Females, on the other hand, will refrain from physical forms of aggression and will lean toward shunning, ostracizing, and defaming others.

- *What can you do?* In younger children, parents should be positive and consistent in their modeling correct behaviors, and nurturing in order to teach appropriate coping skills and offering support and ways the child can express their frustrations in more acceptable ways vs. aggressive, hostile, and antisocial acts upon others. Let the child know that the inappropriate behavior(s) will not be tolerated and that they have appropriate choices and methods that they may use when feeling frustrated. Any time an aggressive action results in the destruction of property and/or hurting another, the child will need to review his/her actions, apologize, and make restitution for the damages.

- *Extreme Cases:* Some children will obviously be more difficult to assist in modifying their aggressive tendencies than others. In such instances, it is best to maintain a journal or log of the triggers resulting in aggressive behavior. I utilized this extensively within my classroom and it allowed me to recognize situations in advance, before they escalated out of control. Share the information that you obtain with the child's parents and/or caregiver to determine if they notice similar triggers at home. Certain aspects that we aren't aware of can actually be causing the frustration. For instance, the environment in which your child spends a great deal of time can actually be causing anxiety for the child. Perhaps the room arrangement is unacceptable to the child's need to have freedom to move about without obstructions, maybe he/she feels crowded or is claustrophobic, or maybe he/she just needs more time to move about freely without being required to sit for extended periods of time. Believe it or not, this can be quite difficult for children. If you're a teacher, I'd recommend preparing a plan of action which specifies consequences for the child's negative behaviors should they occur. Establish a list of acceptable activities that the child can call upon in the event of frustration to help calm the child and reduce the likelihood of an aggressive outburst. Recognize success EVERY time the child is able to control his/her aggressive behaviors. Praise him/her for making better choices. It is important that you teach the child calming techniques such as deep breathing and visualization/relaxation exercises. If the child does not respond to your strategies, you may want to consider seeking counseling.

Although our next specific misbehavior can be linked to aggressive behaviors, it doesn't mean that the child will not outgrow the inappropriate response.

Hitting and Biting:

Most typical in infants and toddlers, hitting and biting is another response to frustration and/or stresses that the child is unable to communicate about. Obviously, both can result in a great deal of pain to the victim. Infants, although unaware of the pain they are inflicting, will often bite their mothers. Sometimes this occurs when they are teething and nursing and sometimes for the mere reaction they they'll elicit.

Hitting and biting are both very primitive ways of handling frustration and must be handled in an effort to prevent the behavior from recurring. Often it occurs with little or no warning when a child has reached his/her capacity for handling a situation that is no longer within their control. As parents, teachers and caregivers we must teach children how to maintain control when handling intense emotions.

- Hitting and biting will not go away overnight. In fact, it may increase temporarily while you are attempting to teach the child acceptable and unacceptable methods for dealing with their frustrations. The best way to handle situations such as these would be to wait until a calm moment after the infraction occurs. Discuss why hitting and biting are not acceptable ways to let others know that they are angry and frustrated. Along with the child, demonstrate how ridiculous their actions appear to others. A lot of times when a parent assumes the role of the child and pretends to react inappropriately the same way the child demonstrated moments earlier, they will be able to recognize that they need to handle the situation differently.

- Allow the child to help brainstorm other acceptable alternatives, like perhaps hitting a pillow or squeezing a beanbag; or holding his/her breath and counting to ten or as high as he/she can count (if not up to ten). Whatever you deem appropriate and necessary will assist the child in learning to handle his/her emotions in a better way.

- Teach the child self-soothing methods that can be implemented before he/she explodes. Self-soothing can be anything from removing him/herself from the situation and coloring a picture; perhaps listening to calming music; or even going for a brief walk (depending upon your location). I've even heard of parents and teachers having a specific area for "cooling off." You, too, can establish a "Chill Zone" for times like these. Again, you'll have to customize the approaches to your surroundings.

- Finally, if and when a child has lost control and is unable to calm him or herself, physical restraint is sometimes necessary. When restraining a child (somewhat like a bear hug) you'll want to calmly remind the child that people aren't for hitting and/or biting.

UNDER NO CIRCUMSTANCE SHOULD YOU RESTRAIN A CHILD WITH ANYTHING OTHER THAN YOUR ARMS AND LEGS IF NECESSARY. REMAIN CALM AND DO NOT LET ANGER DICTATE YOUR RESTRAINT.

- Never, ever hit and/or bite the child to teach them that the behavior is inappropriate or painful. This may confuse the child, and certainly may result in feelings of fear of those who they are supposed to trust, respect, admire, and feel comfortable with.

Next on our list of specifics will be that of handling the defiant child. Having to deal with outright disobedience is a job that we all dread, mostly because we've exhausted our toolbox of tricks and have no more ideas about how to handle the situation. When dealing with a defiant child, it seems that it becomes nothing more than a battle of wills. Who has more will... you guessed it - your child. Let's discuss what to do when all else has failed to elicit the desired behavior and/or response from your child.

Dealing with Defiance:

First and foremost, handling misbehavior quickly and consistently is of utmost importance in effectively dealing with this type of behavior. I will share with you eight tried, true, and tested methods of dealing with "super-charged" ugliness.

- Making certain that the child is immediately made aware of your intolerance of his/her behavior, attitude, or action. You want the child to know up front that this behavior is not going to continue and will not be tolerated under any circumstance.

- Consequences must be implemented in order to rectify defiance and one-size-fits-all will not work when dealing with defiant children. So, let's first address *site-specific behaviors* and the removal of the child. For instance, you and your child are in the grocery store and your child keeps taking things from the shelf and placing them into the buggy. You've asked the child politely to replace the items and the child ignores your first, second, and final request. What do you do? Without hesitation and with NO convincing, begging, or threatening on your part, state clearly what you've requested of your child and REMOVE him/her from the area - in this case the store. If the child is small enough, pick him/her up and leave (yes, that means leaving a cart full of items behind - no problem). Children will always try and call a bluff. He/she may begin to whine, scream, kick, and thrash around like a fish out of water as a form of emotional blackmail. If you do not provide the emotional response the child is attempting to elicit the child has no leverage and ultimately receives no payoff. This allows the child to see that you mean business, no matter what. Your ability to maintain your cool is mandatory. Removing your child after specifying clearly that he/she failed to listen to and follow your instructions will make it clear to your child WHO is in control.

- If the behavior is not site-specific, such as a sandbox, playground, classroom learning center, store, sporting event, practice, party, etc., and removal of the child will not be an effective method of handling the defiance, you'll need to create consequences that will motivate and/or inspire your child to behave appropriately. To review more information on establishing consequences, review Part III on Positive Discipline, Accountability, and Consequences. NOTE: As you read the recommended information, pay careful attention to the portion that suggests that the consequences be directly tied to the misbehavior in question - especially the loss of privileges.

- Expanding the consequences is another effective tool in modifying the defiant child's behavior. For instance, your child who is attending a skating party and begins acting out of line is reprimanded and told that as a result of his inappropriate behavior he'll/she'll have to miss the next party. Additionally, as a clever tool, take a photograph of your child misbehaving so that you'll have substance when the next invitation to attend a party arrives. Without allowing your child an opportunity to object to the consequence, you whip out the photo, providing a reminder to your child of his/her misbehavior at the last party and the resulting consequence of missing this party. The child immediately is made aware of your intent to follow through as well as the recognition that it was his/her behavior that elicited the consequence.

- Count down is another method of handling defiant children, but only if you will follow through when you reach the target number. Parents who utilize this method indicated that counting backwards with zero as the final number is more effective than using five, six, and seven as the destination. Although with younger children this is effective, I prefer to provide older children with a time limit in order to allow them to complete whatever they are doing, within reason. For instance, an older child that is playing a card game who has been instructed to take-out the garbage. Obviously, accommodating your child while respecting the fact that he/she is involved in a game is something you want to do, while at the same time making the child aware that you will not wait and/or be tolerant of the game lingering. By establishing a reasonable time frame (for example, in this case five minute windows), within which the child MUST take out the garbage, you've reduced the occurrence of defiance as the child will recognize your empathy and consideration.

- Empathizing with your child, letting him/her know that you understand how he/she must feel and that you recognize that they are frustrated speaks volumes to children. Providing examples to your children of situations in which you've found yourself feeling frustrated and how you handled the situation at hand is a wonderful tool for teaching your child about appropriate solutions to problems. This method will not work for all children, but is certainly worth an attempt, if only to let your children know that you have listened to them and understand what they are attempting to communicate to you. Empathy should be used when and if you feel that there is an underlying reason for your child's defiance and behavior. For example, a child that refuses to get up from a cushion that he is sitting upon when in the presence of others might be an indication that he/she has soiled their pants and is too embarrassed to move. Or perhaps a child that is vehemently opposed to riding the school bus to or from school may be experiencing some type of bullying or abuse and is refusing your insistence to avoid further trauma. If you suspect there is something that your child is reacting too, you need to calm your child and encourage a conversation with him/her.

• Laughing off the behavior as a form of distraction from the bad behavior is a very effective tool when dealing with toddlers. Some children will behave defiantly to gain attention because they simply want attention – whether negative or positive in nature. Turning the negative(s) into positives through the art of distraction is an acceptable way of resolving potentially troublesome behaviors.

• Making deals (a.k.a. bribery) is a form of negotiation which can have both negative and positive outcomes. If parents choose to implement deal making, it should be used sparingly or you will ultimately pay the price. However, if the behavior you are attempting to rectify is predictable behavior, such as wanting a glass of water at bedtime or having a light remain on so he/she can read, perhaps a small negotiation is in order. For instance, your four-year-old wants to sleep in bed with you and your husband each night (big no-no) and promises that if you'll let him, he'll go to sleep right now instead of fighting the fight that you know will ensue. Perhaps allowing your child 15 minutes of "snuggle time" in your bed with the understanding that he'll have to return to his bed in 15 minutes for bedtime is a workable solution. Not only will this allow "settle down" time, but it will provide him the attention that he desires as well as preventing the struggle(s) which will otherwise occur.

- Do nothing, or so it might seem. Sometimes underlying factors such as exhaustion, hunger, or illness can make even the most easygoing children more like dealing with a hungry bear in that no matter what, they will be unruly and out-of-control. Occasionally this type of behavior will occur when you are unable to do anything about it, such as when you're stuck in traffic, or perhaps in the middle of a doctor's appointment. Remaining calm is the key. However, when you are in a position to handle the matter, handle it. Consequences should be enforced regardless of the reason for the misbehavior, with a little lesson about how the child could have handled his/her hunger, stomachache, etc., more appropriately the next time.

Sometimes children will effectively deal with their defiance on their own, such as in the case of the child refusing to take a nap although he/she can barely hold themselves upright. Chances are your child will eventually succumb to slumber without you having to lift a finger.

Next to the defiant child, who rates as number 1 on the scale of 1 to 10 (with 1 being the most difficult type of behavior(s) to handle), comes disrespectful behaviors, ranking number two. Whether it be the teenage daughter that rolls her eyes after every word leaving your mouth or the pre-teenage son that calls you stupid when you enforce consequences or tell him "NO" to a request that he's made, it isn't easy to swallow. Respect for authority is highly regarded in every culture even though it is demonstrated in many different ways. Regardless, however, is the fact that disrespect is both hurtful and something that should be dealt with immediately and consistently to modify its use and frequency of use. We will identify several methods for handling children demonstrating disrespectful behavior(s) to you and others.

Disrespectful Behavior:

- *Remain calm.* As difficult as I know this is, it must be done if you intend to handle the situation. Becoming angry, which is probably justified, will ultimately result in making matters worse for both you and your child. Once you've calmed yourself in whatever manner you feel is necessary and effective, you will be ready to respond in a fashion that will be much more productive.

- *Provide feedback.* Tell your child how what he/she has said and/or done makes you feel. Speak calmly and in a soft tone while maintaining eye-contact with your child, providing specifics of his/her infraction such as, "When I asked you to turn off your television you rolled your eyes, said, "Whatever," and continued watching. (Immediately, although using a calm demeanor, turn off the television). This suggests to me that you don't care what I've instructed you to do, and consequently you have hurt my feelings and made me angry." By following the pattern of feedback above, you have identified your child's unacceptable behavior(s); modeled self-control while expressing your feelings of hurt and anger; and made him/her aware of the fact that you aren't going to allow the behavior to continue.

- *Refocus - Stay on Track.* Teenagers sometimes behave disrespectfully in an effort to throw parents, teachers, and caregivers off track. They believe that by flustering you when you're telling them or requesting them to do something, you'll forget about the original request and be forced to deal with the disrespectful behavior. It typically works as parents become disillusioned over "what he just said." Don't be sideswiped or their plot against parenting will be effective. Whatever you do to deal with the disrespectful behavior should be immediately followed by repeating whatever the original request was, i.e., "I'd like for you to pick up and sort your dirty laundry." At this point your child will attempt to engage you in some form of argument by launching disrespectful comments. Remember step one (remain calm). Employ step two (provide feedback), identifying the disrespect and restate your instructions, "I know you'd rather ignore my request to pick up and sort your dirty laundry as you don't feel you should be required to participate in caring for your clothes, but you still need to sort your dirty laundry."

- *Behave like the mature adult that you are and resist the temptation to retaliate.* Anger leads us down a very dark path to destruction. As angry as your child's words and actions will make you, NEVER respond with put-downs or words intended to get even, i.e., "smart mouth," "spoiled rotten brat," etc. Name calling will only worsen the situation and create resentment, which will often justify your teenager calling you names in the first place.

- *Listen to your child.* Although your teenager may have elected to use the wrong approach, tone, and words in expressing him/herself to you, he/she might be attempting to tell you something that has merit. You will want to paraphrase to your child what you've gained from his/her tongue lashing in an effort to turn a confrontation into a conversation. This will show that you are willing to listen to his/her perspective as long as it is handled appropriately in the future.

- *Close the door on this chapter.* After you've handled the situation and apologies have been made or punishments served, do not rehash the event as it will not encourage appropriate behavior. Move forward and focus on the positives. When teenagers see that by communicating in a more meaningful manner, they'll be less likely to be disrespectful.

I've addressed some of the most difficult behavior(s) that challenge even the most knowledgeable, skilled, and trained child behavior specialists - this group including parents and teachers. So let's focus our attention on the last remaining behavior of our top five, temper tantrums.

Temper Tantrums:

Some parents may have never experienced their child throwing a temper tantrum while others may have to deal with them repeatedly throughout the day. **What is a temper tantrum, you may ask?** A temper tantrum is a sudden, unplanned display of anger and frustration. Sometimes tantrums are thrown in an effort to demand attention, while other times it might be thrown because the child is unable to effectively communicate his/her needs.

What does a temper tantrum look like? Temper tantrums, although coming in a variety of displays, frequently involve crying, yelling, swinging arms and legs, falling to the ground, rolling around, kicking, and whatever other attention-grabbing moves and sounds a child can summon from within. Tantrums may last anywhere from 30 seconds to 3 minutes and typically are more intense when they first begin and diminish over time (as the child becomes tired and/or doesn't gain the attention they desire).

In extreme cases, temper tantrums may become violent and/or severe enough that the child will hit, bite, and pinch others with whom they come into contact, although this is typically reserved for parents and caregivers. Children between the age of 1 and 4 are more inclined to throw tantrums, although older children and some adults have been known to do so.

What causes children to have tantrums? Tantrums can be thrown for a variety of reasons, but typically it is a normal response when a child is unable to gain his/her independence or is not able to learn a specific skill, i.e., coloring within the lines; tying his/her shoe; or even buttoning a shirt. There are a lot of factors that can contribute to tantrums, including how tired a child might be, a child's level of stress, and even problems that might stem from physical, mental or emotional issues.

How to handle Temper Tantrums: Tantrums are affected in large part by the responses they get from parents. For example, if a child wants a box of cereal and his/her parent tells them, "No," they go into whiny gear. If the answer is still "No," they throw a full-blown temper tantrum in an effort to gain what they desire. If the parent gives in to the demands of the child throwing a temper tantrum, the child receives the desired reward, thereby reinforcing the tantrum, and the behavior will definitely be repeated.

Effective Methods for Dealing with Tantrums:

- *Ignore the tantrum.* Be aware of the triggers and help your child learn how to deal with the anger and frustration of his/her inability to get their way or do something they are incapable of doing. Allow the child to throw the tantrum if that is the only way to calm them. However, don't acknowledge the tantrum while it is underway (unless your child is in danger of hurting him/herself or others) and this includes watching, making eye contact, or speaking to the child. Upon completion of the tantrum, identify the problem that led to the frustration and tantrum and help your child determine a solution. For instance, if your child was unable to button his/her shirt, practice alongside him/her until they attain success, pointing out that all they needed to do was to let you know the problem when it first occurred so that you could help them before they lost control.

- *Isolate the child.* If you are at home you can either allow the child to throw the tantrum wherever he/she begins OR you can carry the child to a safer location such as a crib, playpen, or his/her room. If you fear for his/her safety, remain close but do not participate.

- *Remain Calm.* A child in the throes of a tantrum is obviously out-of-control on many levels. It is important that you stay firmly in control. Do not react with anger or by yelling or spanking your child as this will heighten the situation. Attempt to ignore the behavior to the greatest extent possible.

- *Teach your child alternatives to tantrums.* Obviously the fewer tantrums you and your child experience the better. Teach your child as quickly as you can following his/her temper tantrum more appropriate behaviors. Talk to your child to determine why he/she was angry or frustrated as obviously the tantrum was a result of anger and/or frustration. Then, concentrate on the tantrum itself, making certain that your child knows that this type of behavior is inappropriate and ineffective and doesn't solve their problem. Model what he/she can do the next time when anger and/or frustration present itself. Role play is an excellent tool in teaching children more appropriate behaviors by demonstrating both unacceptable and acceptable behaviors. In fact, children will enjoy the humor derived from watching you pretend to be them (once they have calmed down, of course). When discussing tantrums, make a point of letting your child know that tantrums are bad - not the child. Children want to do what is right and good. By clearly explaining that tantrums are the wrong thing to do when they are angry, they will have a better understanding of what NOT to do next time. Teach your children alternatives such as how to use their words to express the need for help or to let you know that they are unhappy or angry. Teach younger children how and when to use the phrase, "I'm angry," by having them repeat the phrase after you. Review what he/she will say the next time they become angry to determine if your lesson has been clear to the child.

- **_Preventing tantrums._** After repeated tantrums, you will probably be able to identify certain settings and/or events that lead to your child throwing one. Once you identify the triggers, make a point of speaking to your child prior to the onset. For example, a child that throws a temper tantrum every time you take him/her to preschool will need to be corrected. By talking to your child about the appropriate behavior that you expect from him/her you can potentially eliminate future tantrums. This is tedious and time consuming, but the end result will be well worth it. Example: Explain to your child what you are about to do. "We are going to school in a moment." Next, tell your child the kind of behavior you expect, being positive at all times. "At school today, I know you will remember to use nice words, your inside voice, and use words to tell others how you feel." Followed by what behaviors you do NOT want the child to use. "You will not scream at others or throw things because you are angry. When you do these things you scare others." Your child now knows what is expected of him/her. The next step is to have your child agree to your expectations by having him/her say "yes" to a series of questions such as, "Now, tell me how you're going to behave when you go to school. Are you going to use your inside voice? Wait for his/her answer, which should be, "Yes." If not, begin again. This procedure may have to occur daily until he/she learns that tantrums are unacceptable and will not change the outcome.

The good news is that children grow out of throwing temper tantrums as they learn better coping skills and mature. So be patient. You probably won't go gray-headed at this point - save that for when your child begins dating and driving.

Personal Story: My oldest, now 22, decided to throw a temper tantrum one evening after having witnessed a classmate throw one in preschool. He was 1 - 1/2 years old. He flailed himself onto the floor, began kicking his feet and banging his fists upon the ground, he screamed and attempted to cry, although it was the most fake cry I'd ever heard before. I couldn't help myself and I stood watching in disbelief, laughing out loud. After about 15 seconds, I calmly said to him, "When you're finished, let me know. I'll be in the kitchen eating a cookie." No sooner had the word "cookie" left my mouth, he was up, smiling, and waddling to the kitchen. He never had a temper tantrum again. True story!!!

If you are reading this book in eBook format, you may enjoy the video clip immediately following of a toddler without an audience and what he does when throwing a temper tantrum in order to captivate an audience. It is quite funny and very true. http://www.youtube.com/watch?v=KpSfThUv _pc&NR=1&feature=fvwp

For those of you who have older children, this video clip's for you. The video clip below (taken by an older brother) is of a teenage boy throwing a temper tantrum. The images are disturbing but something that might be helpful in inspiring you to teach your child how to handle anger and frustration at a much younger age. http://www.methodshop.com/2009/06/warcraft-temper-tantrum.shtml

Dealing with challenging behaviors can be extremely frustrating and upsetting (for everyone). Knowing a few tricks to help you prevent and/or reduce their frequency is the key to maintaining your composure and sanity. Remember the first step in handling any situation, whether it is behavior related or responding to an emergency, is to remain calm. When you are calm a child is less likely to continue with his/her over-the-top irrational behavior(s). From a calm disposition you will be able to effectively tackle the problem(s) at hand.

This concludes Part IV of Positive Discipline. In the next part I'll review five behavioral specifics such as: 1) Children that lie; 2) Screaming Children; 3) Children that Frequently Interrupt; 4) Children that Run Away; and 5) Handling Foul Language.

Part Five:
Managing Behavioral Challenges

Before beginning Part V, let's review what we focused upon in Part IV. Last we reviewed Dealing with Specifics (Behaviors, that is!) and reviewed particularly difficult behaviors including Aggressive Behavior; Hitting and Biting; Dealing with Defiance; Disrespectful Behavior; and last, but equally as troublesome, we tackled Temper Tantrums. We identified reasons behind the behaviors and methods of modifying the behaviors.

Every day parents, caregivers, and teachers find themselves in situations in which they've exhausted their bag of tricks in handling some of childhood's toughest behavioral challenges. Finding ourselves unable to effectively manage and/or modify certain behaviors can result in our questioning our capabilities in the position of authority that we've accepted the responsibility to handle. When this happens we begin to second-guess ourselves, and perhaps whether we are competent to handle the very important responsibility and task at hand. Managing behavioral challenges can be a difficult task for anyone, even those trained to handle out-of-the-ordinary situations.

Without further ado, let's tackle another handful of some of childhood's most difficult and challenging attitudes and behaviors, but first let's quickly review what we've covered thus far. In Parts I, II, III, and IV we've reviewed: 1) the necessity and "how to" create an effective discipline plan; 2) we reviewed both creative and logical methods of teaching children to listen to eliminate the need to yell and/or raise one's voice; 3) we've identified the necessity of implementing both natural and logical consequences in order to teach children how to be accountable and to teach more appropriate and acceptable behaviors; 4) we tackled 5 of the most difficult behavioral challenges and how to defuse the situations to provide a calm environment in which to teach our children how to modify their behaviors. Now we will outline a few additional challenging behaviors that often make adults in charge want to pull out our hair.

First on our list of behaviors we love to hate (or strongly dislike, if you prefer) is "The Screaming Toddler (or child)." Screaming toddlers can be a particularly difficult behavior to handle as it is very difficult to reason with young children. Screaming, although a natural part of the developmental stages children will progress through, can be especially nerve wracking if it occurs in the presence of others because your child is now disturbing people other than you, adding yet another level of frustration to the equation.

Screaming Toddlers (Children):

Children scream for many reasons and herein lay the biggest problem. Is the child screaming to communicate a particular need such as hunger or a dirty diaper? Or is he/she screaming to receive something that they cannot or shouldn't have like a soda or piece of candy? Your child could be screaming to gain your attention simply because he/she wants it or even just to get a reaction out of you. Whatever the reason, here are a few basics to keep in mind should you find yourself with an out-of-control screamer and not enough cotton to plug your ears to muffle the sound(s):

- **Never Retaliate.** Remember, you are an adult even though you may be in tears. Screaming back at your child will not accomplish the desired outcome. In fact, it may increase the desire of your child to scream louder and longer as if a competition is underway.

- **Distraction.** Children can be distracted somewhat easily and this tool is usually effective. For instance, your child screams a blood-curdling whine because he/she has seen and desperately wants a bag of un-healthy potato chips. By acknowledging his/her desire but suggesting another healthier alternative you can likely silence the child. However, your first attempt at distraction may be unsuccessful so be prepared to move onto Plan B, you know, like, "Look, there's a _____ over there behind the tree, shelf, counter, etc..." Be creative, spontaneous and enthusiastic and go looking for whatever you've pointed out.

- **Be Prepared.** A Boy Scout motto and one that we should all live by. It is always wise to have a special "outing bag" or Bag of Tricks with snacks, drinks and special toys just for use when traveling or running errands with the intention of keeping them captivated.

- **Schedule.** It's always a good idea to plan outings and activities around your child's nap and eating schedule. A full tummy and well rested child is less likely to misbehave.

- **Involve your Children.** Including your children when completing tasks and errands allows them to feel a part of the action and keeps them engaged and much less likely to act out. This can be as simple as allowing the child to depress the "unlock button" to the car or even walk first through the automatic opening doors. Little things make a big difference to kids.

- **Family Friendly Places.** If possible, choose destinations that your child will enjoy. For instance, a pizza joint will probably be more kid friendly and allow for a noisy toddler better than a hoity toity more formal restaurant.

- **Indoor Voice.** Teaching your child to use an indoor voice is one of the best things a parent and teacher can do. When toddlers begin to wind-up for a screaming session, sometimes all you have to do is ask them to be quiet and to use their indoor voice.

- **Stay Calm.** Modeling a calm voice and quiet tone will set a good example for your child. In situations which include screaming children, remaining calm will prevent you from making the situation worse. As difficult as this can be to achieve, it is well worth it.

- **Bail.** If all else fails and none of the techniques above are successful, you may have to remove you and your child from the area - even if it means leaving a cart full of groceries behind. Sometimes a hasty retreat is necessary.

- **Acknowledge but NEVER give in.** When a toddler is out-of-control, acknowledge their feelings in an effort to help them work through the moment. But, unless you are willing to set precedence and encourage a repetition of this song and dance, do not give into the demands of your child.

This stage will ultimately end, but at the moment is likely to result in frazzled nerves and perhaps a gray hair or two.

Another equally disturbing behavior that children around the globe will practice is interrupting. You know the typical scenario. You'll be on the phone with someone when your child who has been playing quietly suddenly has a life or death situation and begins interrupting your conversation. Need I say more? What I will do is provide some tips on what you can do to eliminate this recurring behavior.

Children Who Interrupt:

First let me say that you should expect that your child is going to interrupt you at some point; after all, he's a kid and that's his job. Knowing how to handle and defuse the situation is yours.

Children will begin interrupting you, it seems, the moment they are mobile, preventing your escape to another room. So being prepared is the key. A few tricks and tips will typically resolve the problem, sometimes even before it occurs. Try these:

- **Distractions.** Amazingly enough, again, this is one technique that works on young children MOST of the time. A favorite toy, delicious snack, basket full of interesting "child safe" gadgets, etc., that can be introduced when needed.

- **Teaching Cues.** This is most effective when you begin teaching polite cues as soon as your child begins to talk. The purpose is to teach your toddler a nonverbal way to gain your attention without the use of words, i.e., placing a hand on your knee; tapping you gently on the shoulder, or touching you upon the cheek. Make certain you also teach an "*acknowledgment cue*" to let your child know that you are aware of his/her desire to "speak" or that they need you, but they'll need to wait a moment. In my classroom I acknowledged my students by making eye contact and raising my pointer finger to signal them that I'd be a moment longer. This was also used when in the middle of a lesson and a child felt compelled to interrupt or interject his/her comments and/or opinion and was successful 99% of the time.

- **Polite vs. Impolite Interruptions.** Polite interruptions should be recognized quickly and dealt with promptly as your child is following protocol. By handling the needs of the child who has demonstrated polite interrupting techniques, you are reinforcing the desired behavior. Handling rude interruptions like nagging, yelling, or hitting your arm should be handled with consequences (unless a true emergency exists), i.e., the dire need for a cookie will not be rewarded with a cookie but instead with a time-out.

- **Politely Respond.** When you calmly respond to your child's interruption they feel important and understood. If your child interrupts it is best to maintain your composure and model the polite way to respond to others. By blasting your child about being rude and interrupting you, you've actually modeled "rude" behavior or the incorrect type of behavior that your child will inevitably use in the future.

- **Ask Adults to Wait.** If you are talking to another adult and your child has politely sought your attention, excuse yourself from the conversation at hand to address the needs of your child. Make certain that your child overhears you politely requesting that the other party hold for a moment as it is a teachable moment from which your child can learn.

- **Long-Term Plan for Teaching Manners.** Every parent, caregiver and teacher should have a clear plan for 1) Teaching Manners and Expectations; 2) How they intend to teach and reinforce the proper use of manners; 3) Understanding that in order for children to use manners they must be taught them via modeling and role play.

Children learn positive traits through constant exposure to behaviors and attitudes from their parents, peers, caregivers and teachers. Understanding developmental limitations of children must be taken into account if you want any plan to be successful. It's wise to understand that patience is a virtue during the egocentric years in a child's development.

Equally as frustrating as the child that interrupts every time you open your mouth, but on a different level, is the child that frequently uses foul language. We are all guilty of using a "bad" word from time to time, and although we try our best never to slip up in the presence of a child or children, it happens. Does this make us bad parents? - Absolutely not.

We're human, and like kids we're entitled to make mistakes. The difference lies in the way we handle ourselves upon realization of the errors of our ways.

Dealing with Foul Language:

Let's paint a scenario. You and your family are in a restaurant and your child, age 11, who has apparently learned a new, yet undesirable vocabulary word, uses it in a conversation as though it's as common a word as "then." Your mouth is agape because not only did your family hear it, but the two tables flanking yours heard it too, and suddenly you can hear a pin drop. What do you do? Probably NOT what you are thinking of doing at that very moment - It's probably illegal.

There are many ways of handling this type of behavior - you'll need to decide what works best with the moral character and standards that you have in place for your family. Here are a few age appropriate tips:

- **Try to maintain your composure.** I know in the scenario above this may be extremely difficult, but it is necessary. If the language offends you and your family, discuss this with the child and set limits. Everyone has to learn that certain language may be acceptable to some, but not to others. Your teen can be using bad language for a number of reasons. One of them may be to simply push your buttons. Teens like to feel that they are in control and by swearing in front of their parent(s) they are simply testing the boundaries, seeing exactly how far they can go. Sometimes teens just need to have the boundaries set for them in a clear manner. (Remember, if parents speak rudely, shout and swear at their children and each other, the children will do the same.) After discussing the matter above, have the child make a meaningful apology to the individuals at the tables that inevitably heard the vulgar word being spoken. Not only will this be difficult, but it might require a little prompting on your part. However, the discomfort that your child experiences at this moment may be just what it takes to prevent this from occurring in the future.

- **Discuss Alternative Expressions.** Bad language is not okay for a child, adolescent, or teen to use, and finding the right way to stop the language may be tough. However, it can be done. It's just about finding the right way, like coming up with crazy words to be used instead of the inappropriate word(s). Although I cannot use explicit vulgar words in my writings as examples, I'll provide polite phrases used in lieu of hurtful, rude, or insulting statements instead. Neither I, nor my students, were allowed to say the words "shut up" for many reasons, because it was considered inappropriate and rude. Instead we used the phrase "quiet please" or "please be quiet." Obviously, I'm attempting to make an example with alternatives to inappropriate language instead of obscenities, but I believe you understand the point that I'm attempting to make.

- **Ignore the word.** Especially with younger children who choose to use words that they've heard elsewhere, it is sometimes best to have less of a reaction in an effort to provide less incentive for the child to use it again. At a later point in time, discuss with your child why the word is inappropriate and shouldn't be used.

- **Apply Consequences.** This one is pretty simple and DOES NOT involve a bar of soap or hot sauce. If the child uses inappropriate vocabulary after repeated reminders by you and/or others, consequences may be in order. For example, some parents choose to have a "cuss jar" which earns money every time a person uses an inappropriate word. This is pretty effective with older children as they don't like giving their money away. Another effective tool would be to enforce logical consequences, such as in the event of the teenager that finds it "cool" to use bad language when in the presence of certain friends. Obviously, preventing the child from "hanging" with the individuals that participate in the use of bad language will encourage improved choices in words if he/she intends to ever associate with this friend(s) again. Another consequence might be to have the child find alternative words via dictionary, thesaurus, or online that can be used instead of the offensive word chosen. Perhaps make him/her come up with a list of twenty alternatives and write their definitions.

Using offensive language will ultimately catch up with your child if the habit is not broken. Parents should really take a stand in preventing and/or eliminating the use of bad language at home.

Every parent on the planet, at some point in time, must deal with the frustration associated with back talk, some more than others. It becomes a real problem when parents are unable to maintain their composure, leading to an increased level of anger, which increases the level of insolence from children. With the tips below, you should be successful at controlling the cycle.

Handling Back Talk:

If you grew up in my home you learned very quickly that ANY form of communication when either being directed to do or not to do something was considered back talk, a.k.a. insolence. It wasn't until I was grown and gone that my dad acknowledged this error in his ways and admitted that he should have provided us an opportunity to express our opinion or objection without it being considered back talk. However, because we weren't provided that opportunity, oftentimes he received back talk as we attempted to assert our opinions. As frustrating as it was for him, and is for many parents, here are a few suggestions to decrease the opportunity for your child to behave rudely in the form of back talk:

- **Remain calm and do not overreact.** If we present a calm demeanor our children are less likely to escalate. However, should the interaction take on the form of a shouting match, everyone should take a timeout in order to calm down. Once this is accomplished, address the disrespectful talk that your child has demonstrated, explaining how it is ineffective as a method of communicating and why you will not tolerate such disobedience.

- **Be a good role model.** If you model disrespect in front of your children when communicating with anyone, your children will learn to communicate disrespectfully - guaranteed.

- **Consistent "play book" for back talk.** You should establish a routine that you can live with in order to eliminate the frequency of back talk from your children. For instance, providing your child one warning and the opportunity to modify their disrespectful behavior might be in order. However, if your child continues to treat you with disrespect by continuing the back talk, enforcing appropriate consequences are in order. While young children will respond well to time out, older children will need something more suitable to the situation, i.e., if the back talk is about remaining out later with his/her friends, perhaps requiring him/her to be home an hour earlier to think about their level of disrespect is appropriate and more effective. Or perhaps not allowing him/her to participate in the chosen activity with friends at all is more suitable. It really depends on what you feel is going to be the most effective at reducing or eliminating back talk in your home. Remember; recognize the positive behaviors when your children speak respectfully in an effort to provide reinforcing more of the desired behavior(s) within your home.

- **Use "I" Statements.** When speaking to your child about his/her disrespectful behavior, using "I" statements to explain how your child makes you feel is a very powerful tool. For example, "When you speak to me in a disrespectful tone and mumble words of anger under your breath, I become hurt and frustrated." Statements such as this will clearly make the point to your child while modeling positive communication skills, which is ultimately what we are attempting to teach them to do when communicating with us and others.

Back talk is angry, impulsive behavior. And although we want our children to be able to express their opinions and even their objections, we want them to do so in a respectful manner. Preventing a child from communicating his/her thoughts is actually teaching a child that his/her thoughts don't matter and this can lead to outbursts of frustration from your child.

Teaching a child how to calmly express their thoughts and opinions utilizing self-censorship is important and will impact how he'll/she'll get along with others in the future. Reducing and ultimately eliminating back talk will take practice and time. By remaining calm and consistent you will be able to squelch this troublesome behavior.

Effectively communicating with your children and providing an opportunity for them to express their desires, fears, concerns, opinions, and objections is a necessary element of teaching children to be respectful. It also maintains an open line of communication for your child if and when they feel a need to discuss matters that are particularly difficult for them to address. As parents we want our children to feel safe, comfortable, and secure enough to come to us when it matters. When we exude a closed mind mentality, or demonstrate greater anxiety levels when handling particularly troublesome behaviors with our children, we unknowingly encourage them to go elsewhere with their problems and concerns or influence them to be dishonest with us, typically in the form of a lie. Let's address the art of lying.

Why Children Lie
and How to Discourage It:

People lie for a multitude of reasons. In children, however, it seems that the common denominator is fear. Fear of what, you might be asking yourself? Let's find out:

- Children will employ a big, fat, hairy lie when they are scared of the consequences for their actions. As parents, we should immediately review the circumstances surrounding their constant need (or feeling the need) to lie. Are our rules too strict? Are our limits too tight? And most importantly, does our child feel comfortable and/or free to talk to us about ANYTHING?

- Children will often lie to protect somebody else with whom they share loyalty.

- Sometimes children will create "tall tales" in order to make the boring seem unbelievable (which typically parents can deduce).

- Children will be dishonest to avoid unpleasant tasks, i.e., "Did you clean your fish tank?"... "Yes, Mom!"

- Oftentimes children will lie almost by accident as a lie at certain points in time come more naturally than the truth. Yes, it is usually to cover a misdeed of sorts. For example, "Did you break the window?" "I didn't," is a typical response - even if they did.

- Some children will lie if they think it will elicit love, approval, or increase their popularity, if only for a moment. An example of this would be the child that creates unbelievable stories regarding fame, fortune, etc...

Now that I've identified a lot of the reasons that children will lie, what can we as parents, teachers, and caregivers do to prevent this type of behavior and encourage a child to always tell the truth? Even though you can't keep your child from lying, discouraging it can be accomplished in a few simple ways.

- **Don't Play the Blame Game.** Instead of focusing on the "blame" for an event that has taken place, try to center your conversation upon what happened and/or what the problem is. Children who aren't fearful of being blamed will usually tell the truth.

- **Leave Cross-Examining for the Courtroom.** Sometimes parents and teachers get bogged down with asking too many details. Remember, the object is to encourage your child to communicate. Interrogating your child will lead to him/her shutting down instead of opening up to you.

- **Positive Intent.** When talking with your child, try to determine the underlying reason for the lie. Lies are typically associated with a misguided attempt for survival.

- **Avoid laying a trap.** If your child has misbehaved, avoid setting him/her up by forcing them into a no-win situation. Avoid using leading questions, or creating a situation in which your child feels the only way to survive is to lie. For instance, your child comes home from school with a black eye. You immediately lose your composure and confront him with, "If you got into a fight at school you'll be spending your weekend in your room." This is ineffective in opening up the lines of communication. Why? 1) Your child is now backed into a corner. Forget the fact that he was protecting himself from the class bully, because now he feels that he's got to protect himself from you by telling you a lie. "No, I walked into an opened locker." A better, much more effective method would be, "Uh oh! What happened? Let's put some ice on it and sit down and talk about it." By handling matters in a more composed, compassionate manner, you might actually find out that your child is being bullied and really needs some constructive advice and perhaps intervention.

- **Telling the truth can be EXTREMELY difficult.** For some, telling the truth is as easy as telling a lie. For others, it's almost as difficult as childbirth. It's taking a risk. The risk being: 1) your reaction; 2) the consequence. As a teacher and mother, I made a deal with my children that I would always tell them the truth - no matter what. It is a reciprocal deal in that they must always tell me the truth - no matter what – we shook fingers, making a "Pinky Promise." As strange as this may seem, it has been very effective and beneficial in my relationship with my sons, who are now grown young men and able to come to me with ANYTHING. My philosophy may not work for you, so in the event that your child swallows his/her fear and comes clean there are two important steps you should take. 1) Thank your child for telling the truth, providing positive reinforcement for exercising his/her excellent moral compass; 2) Handle the misdeed by applying appropriate consequences. In fact, when a child has been truthful, including them in determining an appropriate consequence is extremely beneficial in encouraging the behavior again. In order for this plan to be successful you MUST do Step 1 followed by Step 2. Otherwise, your child will likely NOT correct the behavior. Positive feedback for telling the truth MUST be consistent just as consistency in the use of consequences must be. By focusing first on the positive(s) your child will be better accepting of the consequences.

- **Never reprimand your child for telling the truth.**

- **False Accusations.** Children are devastated when they've been falsely accused. So, to prevent this from occurring make certain that you are clear on the details that have been shared with you. As you can imagine, if your child is telling you the truth and you do not believe him/her and do not support him/her, there will be a less likely chance of your child communicating with you in the future.

As was mentioned in several of my books, children are tricky little creatures and sometimes we find ourselves at the end of our wits when handling situations that arise. As a parent, teacher, or caregiver, knowing the traps and/or pitfalls within which we can easily tumble is extremely important. We must educate ourselves so that we can teach our children. I'm here to help you do just that. Hopefully I can take the edge off by providing you the tips and strategies to manage your home and effectively teach your children how to become self-disciplined adults.

Thank you for taking the time to read and review Part V of Positive Discipline. The next segment I'll be sharing is Behavior Management, Part IV t's just as informative as the previous sections, but it takes discipline into the classroom.

NOTE: Although we didn't specifically touch upon children that whine, whining can be a part of the "screaming toddler" syndrome. If you have a whiner - attached is a video instructing parents how to modify this type of behavior. Just click and watch. http://www.monkeysee.com/play/4185-what-else-can-parents-do-to-discourage-whining

Part Six:
Behavior Management in Schools

Last but certainly not least, Part VI of Positive Discipline is Behavior Management in Schools. Thanks for joining me for Discipline 101, Part VI: Behavior Management in Schools. This tends to be an area of particular concern for many parents, teachers, children, and caregivers. For parents it is frustrating because we choose to live in areas, within our financial means, where our children will be able to obtain the best education possible. Often this means a higher mortgage payment and higher property taxes than others may pay. For teachers, spending the majority of any day dealing with misbehavior or annoying behavior(s) can result in the loss of enjoyment within the classroom, especially if you always feel like you're going into battle immediately upon opening the door. And believe it or not, for children it can be just as frustrating. The child that enjoys school and learning must often wait for the teacher to deal with discipline concerns. This "waiting game" can seem like hours, and sometimes it is, especially when you calculate the time wasted daily handling classroom disruptions.

For the child constantly being ignored and required to wait, learning can become less rewarding, sometimes resulting in the child losing interest, while others, children who are typically well-behaved, may actually begin to misbehave in an effort to gain some of the teacher's attention for themselves.

Something must be done to allow those who want to learn an opportunity to learn without the constant disruptions, and the teacher an opportunity to teach without spending the majority of his/her time handling disruptions.

In previous segments, we focused on dealing with specific behaviors and reviewed particularly difficult behaviors including aggressive behavior; hitting and biting; dealing with defiance; disrespectful behavior; and last, but equally as troublesome, we tackled temper tantrums. I identified reasons behind the behaviors and methods that can be implemented to modify the behaviors.

Every day, teachers find themselves in situations in which they've exhausted their bag of tricks in handling some of childhood's toughest behavioral challenges. These challenges are NOT just limited to elementary-aged children, but more often than not include middle school and high school-aged children as well. Where most elementary teachers can modify misbehaviors through re-directing the attention and focus of their students, the upper levels are often more difficult to manage. Finding ourselves unable to effectively manage and/or modify certain behaviors can result in us questioning our capabilities in the position of authority that we've accepted the responsibility to handle. When this happens we begin to second-guess ourselves and perhaps whether we are competent to handle the very important responsibility and task at hand. Managing behavioral challenges can be a difficult task for anyone, even those trained to handle out-of-the-ordinary behaviors. So just imagine, like teachers do every day, being in a classroom full of potential behavior challenges.

This segment will focus on behavior management in schools and more specifically the classroom. Now, as any teacher knows, classroom management begins not only with a clear and concise set of standards and expectations that you intend for your students to adhere to, but is also dependent upon other criteria such as furniture layout and functionality. I addressed classroom management in my book series, *Children Topics from A to Z: A Guide for Tackling Tough Issues* in a topic entitled "Effective Classroom

Management." Upon completion of this segment, you may choose to read that topic to obtain additional information on the subject.

Four Fundamentals of Effective Classroom Management

An effective classroom management plan should include four fundamentals:

1. Know what you want and what you don't want – make this clear to your class full of students AND their parents.

2. Show and tell your students what you want. Especially in the lower grades, where modeling your expectations and involving your students in role-play is a great tool for getting the point(s) across, leaving minimal room for misinterpretation by your students.

3. When you get what you want, acknowledge it. Acknowledging the behaviors that you want your students to engage in will encourage other students to engage in the appropriate behaviors as well.

4. When you get something else, act quickly and appropriately. Obviously this step is extremely important and should take into account the individual temperament(s) of the students involved. Handling a child inappropriately or with the wrong tone will often send the child off the deep end, making the situation that you originally addressed feel like a walk in the park.

Let me begin by briefly reviewing the first area of concern and which is considered by many educators to be a proactive measure in reducing potential misbehavior(s) within your classroom.

Classroom Layout and Arrangement:

Most teachers will agree that while a carefully thought out and planned classroom arrangement is not a guarantee of good behavior by their students, poor planning in this areas or a failure to plan at all can create conditions that lead to problems. Keeping this in mind, here are a few tips to help reduce complications from an ineffective floorplan.

I'll call them the Five Foundations to a Solid Footing:

- A teacher's desk should always be positioned in order to allow her visibility of all students at all times. This allows for the proper monitoring of work habits and behavior. Additionally, placement of the desk to allow for visibility of the door(s) is mandatory.

- Insure that areas of the classroom that will receive a great deal of traffic are unobstructed by desks, chairs, or other furniture, including trash cans and water fountains.

- Proper arrangement of student tables or desks should allow for a clear view of presentation(s) and/or instruction without unnecessary movement or turning.

- Classroom materials and supplies should be placed in an area readily accessible by all students and easily monitored by the teacher.

- Classrooms that are lacking decorations and color become dreaded places for students and teachers. Much like the time spent decorating your home, bedroom, or office space, classrooms should receive attention to details to make them colorful, attractive and desirable.

Our second area, and definitely equally as important as the previous, is establishing your expectations and making certain that your students understand what is allowed or not allowed, appropriate and inappropriate.

Establishing Student Expectations:

Students will not walk into your class knowing who you are and what you expect of them. Perhaps they've come from a class with an entirely different "expectation agenda" than you'll entertain within your classroom. Making students aware that you have expectations for each individual and clearly communicating your expectations is necessary. And don't think that you can explain them only once (although in a perfect world we'd all like to believe that to be true). Repeating your expectations periodically will assist your students in internalizing them and then meeting or exceeding them.

- Establish classroom rules and then post them. Students are a wonderful help in developing classroom rules. By allowing them to participate in their establishment, they are already committed to them. Therefore, they will be less likely to violate a rule or procedure intentionally. Monitoring the rules will need to be consistent without vacillating. NOTE: Never establish rules that you are unwilling to uphold or enforce.

- Some schools have school-wide regulations. These school-wide rules typically include safety procedures that will be implemented should there be a school-wide emergency and/or drill. We're pretty familiar with fire and tornado drills, but there are also "lock down" procedures used in schools should a person of concern enter the school. Please insure students know what to do in the event of an emergency to help reduce the risk of chaos or unnecessary harm or injury.

- Misbehavior or "off-task" behavior often occurs during activities and transitions from one activity or location within the school to another. By instructing your students prior to the activity or transition as to your expectations, I mean painting a clear picture for them to visualize, you can reduce the number and frequency of disruptions and increase a smoothly functioning classroom and/or transition.

- Clearly establishing a daily routine and practicing it without modification (unless absolutely necessary) is key to maintaining a well-managed classroom and learning environment. This begins the minute the children first enter the classroom each day and focuses on attendance, lunch procedures, obtaining materials and supplies, and homework submittal to obtaining homework assignments at the end of the day upon dismissal. Included in the procedures should be sharpening pencils, storing their belongings, obtaining supplies, and the need to use the restroom or get water. By taking the time to review the daily procedures with your students, including what they are permitted to do and what they may not engage in during specific times, you'll set the stage for a carefully managed group of students.

- Students should be aware of the procedures as they relate to both teacher-led instruction and seatwork. Obviously if you are instructing the students on the "how to's" of something, the last thing you want is an interruption of a child going to sharpen his/her pencil, etc. By making students aware of the appropriate times in which they can handle particular needs, you are making it less likely to occur during inappropriate times.

- Part of establishing expectations is to teach your children how you'd like them to respond when desiring to answer questions, or to gain your attention using a "polite interrupting cue." As mentioned in the previous section, teaching cues to politely gain your attention as well as cues to be used as a response is necessary if you don't want to entertain interruptions throughout the day. Obviously many teachers will encourage raising a hand and this works fine. But, establishing a response cue so that the teacher can complete his/her sentence or finish the point he/she is trying to get across needs to be addressed and taught to make this important task possible.

Teachers should remember that good discipline is much more likely to occur in the classroom setting if activities are structured or arranged to enhance cooperative behavior.

Obviously the main purpose of attending school is for learning. So, it is important to have a plan for managing student academic work. This portion of effective behavior management is strongly the responsibility of the teacher.

Managing Student Academic Work:

In any classroom, effective teacher-led instruction is free from:

- The use of vague terms. Students need clear and concise instruction, and insuring that each child is able to understand what is being relayed is important. Simply stating what you might think is obvious one way is quite likely to be confusing to more than one student. Repeating your instruction using various descriptions of the content being taught as well as the expectations of your students will help to prevent frustration among your students and reduce and/or eliminate potential distractions and misbehavior.

- Unclear or illogical sequencing. Your instructions needs to make logical sense in order for your students to grasp the meaning and/or steps that you'd like them to take in completing an assignment or transitioning from one activity/location to another. When driving, there is a logical sequence and process that a driver will take to get from point A to point B. This is true in the classroom as well.

- Unnecessary interruptions. In any environment, reducing the number of interruptions will improve your ability to remain on task and prevent unnecessary delays in instruction. Plan times throughout your daily routine for your students to get water, use the restroom, and/or obtain the information that is needed to complete a project, assignment, or task.

Students should always be held accountable for their work or lack thereof. If a child doesn't complete an assignment and submit it following the established criteria, a consequence should certainly follow. This is not to say, of course, that a reminder should not be utilized to encourage the child to follow protocol and turn his/her work in as necessary. But, should the child fail to follow the required procedures after providing reminders and even warning(s), he/she should be penalized accordingly.

Although good behavior is necessary and important in its own right, make certain that students understand that the primary focus in attending school is on the academic tasks that they are presented and completion of the assignments that follow. Effort is everything in the classroom.

Alongside that of managing academic work within the classroom lies the largest concentration of a teacher's time these days. It is unfortunate that a once-cherished experience has become tarnished with the "fog" we often find ourselves within.

Handling Inappropriate Behaviors:

- For most teachers, using a cue or simple verbal reprimand is all it takes to redirect a student's focus, reducing or eliminating the inappropriate behavior that he/she has elected to participate in. However, sometimes these measures are ineffective at obtaining the desired behavior. Additionally, however, use of praise recognizing the efforts of the majority vs. the minority is also very effective at redirecting the off-task and/or disruptive student. Should these efforts be unsuccessful for the child that frequently disrupts the class and/or other students, an individualized contract identifying the disruptive behavior and a method of encouraging the desired behavior should be considered. Typically this includes a consequence for the specific misbehavior that has been identified, which eliminates the need to start from square one every time the child violates the rule or procedure. This is only effective if there is a reward or recognition for the student meeting or obtaining the agreed upon goal, so remember to include the positives too.

- As a teacher who is obviously focused on his/her students, reading verbal cues can help to eliminate or prevent interruptions and/or misbehavior from occurring. If you notice a student becoming frustrated with an assignment or project, addressing the situation and intervening as quickly as possible will often prevent an escalation of his/her frustration and resolve the problem at hand. (Note: A teacher should put down any distractions and keep their eyes focused on their students).

- Teachers should keep a smile on their face throughout the day as this promotes a happy environment and approval of students and their actions and behaviors. However, a teacher should also implement facial cues and/or expressions to signify to students behaviors that aren't appropriate in an effort to let them know they are being watched. By making eye contact and moving into close proximity with the offending student that is bordering on potentially off-task and/or disruptive behavior(s), a teacher can eliminate a lot of the misbehaviors from occurring before they actually do. Teachers that remain behind their desks will find it more difficult to manage classroom discipline problems than teachers that are up and about the classroom and amongst his/her students.

- Sometimes a teacher will have to single out the offending students when other non-verbal attempts have been unsuccessful. For instance, a teacher calling a student by name and giving a short verbal instructtion to stop a specific behavior, such as tapping a pencil, whistling, or even making noises, will often eliminate the behavior. However, sometimes it will become necessary to redirect the student by reciting applicable procedures and/or rules. An example of this would be during instruction, "Please look at the overhead projector and read the first line with me, and I need to see everyone's eyes looking here."

- We unfortunately experience more aggressive and disrespectful behaviors within our schools and classrooms these days, including fighting, continuous interruption of lessons, stealing, the use of profanity, and possession of drugs. These offenses are typically handled at another level and are normally outlined by the school board within a school system. The consequences required are usually more extreme than those implemented within the classroom.

Assertive discipline is an effective tool for handling much misbehavior within our schools and classrooms. I'll be addressing this below.

Promoting Appropriate Use of Consequences:

- Within the classroom and typically shared by most children is the use of positive consequences. These consequences are intrinsic in nature and occur via student satisfaction resulting from his/her success, accomplishment, good grades, social approval, and recognition for his/her efforts.

- Students need to be taught the connection between the proper completion of tasks and grades. By making students aware of how their efforts to complete a particular assignment and/or prepare for a test will directly influence the outcome they are made aware that it is their responsibility that will ultimately determine the outcome.

- Teachers that frequently use punishment within their classrooms in an effort to gain control of their students can be linked to poor classroom management skills and will prove ineffective in the long run. This type of classroom management should be discouraged and should be replaced with more positive effective management techniques.

- When students misbehave, the consequence should "fit the crime." In other words, using logical and/or natural consequences will be much more effective at obtaining the desired behavior(s) the next time around. By making the penalty logical it is less likely to be met with negative emotion. Sure, your student won't be thrilled with serving a time-out or missing a class field trip, but they are more capable of recognizing the errors of their ways when serving a punishment that makes sense.

- Consistency in the classroom (and at home) is mandatory in teaching children the differences between right and wrong, appropriate vs. inappropriate, and acceptable and unacceptable behaviors. This includes consistency both in making the children adhere to the established rules and routines as well as applying consequences should they not. By providing counseling to the child that frequently misbehaves in the form of one-on-one consultations and/or group meetings reviewing the desired behaviors, a child can be encouraged to make a commitment to avoid the actions that typically land him/her in "hot water" and focus on participating in more desirable alternative behaviors and activities.

Although there are literally hundreds of annoying classroom distractions that can disrupt classroom proceedings, let's review the top seven areas deserving specific notice and what can be done to reduce, prevent, and/or eliminate them:

1. Antagonism with Authority:

- By providing students the opportunity for students to change their hostile and aggressive energy into more socially acceptable channels such as sports, clubs, crafts, hobbies, etc., you'll encourage them to be less insubordinate. When I was in the classroom I found that everyone, including me, needed an occasional opportunity during the day to just be themselves. As a group we participated in activities, games, outside play, or sports that gave us the much needed break and reflected my concern for their emotional health too.

- Read literature or require reading/writing assignments that deal with antagonistic behaviors and ask them to identify different socially acceptable ways of handling conflict situations.

- Discuss with the student in private what it is that motivates him/her to misbehave.

- Provide models of more appropriate communicative behavior through role-playing and discussion(s).

- Although I'd like to believe that there is no difference, emphasize to students that there may be a difference in the way that they communicate at home and at school. Perhaps model the differences using children as participants and provide scenarios for them to act out.

- Refer the student, if necessary, to staff members that are in place to help with out-of-the-ordinary situations, i.e. school counselor, student support team, etc.

- Contact parents and/or administrators when you are ineffective at resolving the conflict.

2. Argumentative Student:

- Never confront a student that is demonstrative of argumentative behavior in the presence of a group. This will provide him/her an audience and really set the stage for a performance.

- When addressing a student, avoid using an accusatory tone, which can escalate the tension, resulting in a more difficult situation.

- Review the situation and events leading up to the incident/confrontation.

- Allow the student to calm him/herself. Never back a student into a corner. They must feel that there are options available.

- Avoid making statements and/or threats that cannot be measured or carried out.

- If you find yourself agitated, allow yourself to calm down before approaching the student.

- Allow the student an opportunity to speak his/her piece. By eliminating an opportunity for communication, you eliminate the opportunity for the child to explain and/or apologize if an apology is in order.

- Depending upon the age of the child, engage your student in role reversal and role play in an effort to allow him/her to see how he/she behaved.

- Most importantly, if you offended your student and/or were wrong, you'll need to admit it and offer an apology. It works both ways.

3. Behavior Problems:

- Meet with the student that demonstrates inappropriate behaviors and explain in exact terms the behaviors that are unacceptable in the classroom. Include WHY the behaviors are inappropriate. You will always want to insure that the child understands that it is his/her BEHAVIOR that is unacceptable and not the child.

- Readdress the problem and let the student know what to expect (consequence) should the problem continue or re-occur.

- Should the problem occur again, immediately follow-through with the disciplinary action presented in advance.

- Always make certain that you keep the parents and your administrator informed of the progress or lack thereof.

- In the event that the child continues to misbehave and you've exhausted your bag of tricks, sending the child to the office for further action is in order. Explain to the child that if he/she is capable of following the classroom rules, he/she can return. NOTE: With younger children, planning a special event, treat, free-time, etc., is very effective when the violating child is removed from the class. It allows them to see the activities that they will miss due to their constant misbehavior. This works amazingly well to eliminate misbehavior.

4. Boastful, Attention-Seeking Student:

- Some students cannot help themselves and frequently disturb the teacher in an effort to gain attention. Often these children lack the attention that they need and desire at home and are therefore seeking it at school. By providing the student with a position of responsibility, i.e., passing out papers; lunchroom monitor, etc., you can encourage the child to set a good example for others, thereby reducing the inappropriate and distracting attention-seeking behaviors.

- In elementary classrooms, reviewing the "polite cues" for gaining your attention is often necessary and should be repeated regularly. Displaying a poster with the rules is a good idea as they will always be visible by your students.

- Assign the student a special project or assignment and allow him/her to share it with the class, which will often encourage a more appropriate manner in which to receive attention.

- Ignoring the student's inappropriate attention-seeking measures but praising the child for appropriate behaviors and achievements will encourage more appropriate forms of behavior, i.e., "Thank you for preparing your materials for the upcoming quiz."

- Provide recognition and positive attention whenever possible.

- Model the behavior that you want your students to emulate daily so that he/she can see what is expected of him/her. This can also be accomplished through role-playing.

- Schedule a conference with his/her parents to discuss any factors that may be encouraging this type of behavior within the child, e.g., sibling rivalry, low self-esteem, etc.

5. Hyperactivity – Shift in Attention:

- This type of behavior has become all too common in the classroom and can be extremely frustrating, NOT just for the teacher, but for the child that cannot seem to remain focused, frequently gets into trouble as a result, and usually suffers in establishing meaningful relationships with classmates and others. If you have students who are inclined to get off-task and appear unable to remain focused and/or interested in class you can employ a few effective tools. For example, assigning the student with a classroom responsibility that he/she looks forward to completing IF their responsibilities have been met, e.g., collecting completed work, delivering messages, etc.

- Placement of the student's work area should focus on minimizing classroom distractions, i.e., away from windows that allow him to watch everything going on outside; near the water fountain or classroom sink where others will tend to gather.

- Plan individual and/or group assignments that will encourage the development of analytical abilities – such as step-by-step procedures in solving everyday problems.

- Provide your students with firm but fair classroom rules. Make sure you consistently adhere to the consequences for breaking rules.

- Utilize social reinforcements and do so as soon as possible, e.g., physical nearness or contact, a smile or a frown.

- Prepare a variety of shorter lessons to encourage and maximize student attention and participation. Include moments for physical activities to break up the monotony of academics.

6. Lack of Motivation:

- Teachers often have to deal with students that come to class unprepared, lack motivation (or so it seems), and have a negative attitude toward school. This is an area of particular interest to me and one on which I can certainly shine some light. But, before going forward with tips and strategies I need to paint a scenario to make my point. My youngest son, now in the U.S. Coast Guard, was eager to begin kindergarten. Every day throughout the summer he asked if it was time yet. He couldn't wait to start. He was happy, enthusiastic, excited about learning, and friendly to everyone that he met. He always had a smile on his face. One week after being placed into a kindergarten class with a teacher that had no business teaching young children his entire attitude about school changed. In fact, his attitude about living changed. He came home on the third day begging not to have to return. By the fourth day he was pretending to be sick, followed by the fifth day when he uttered the words, "I want to kill myself." Obviously shocked by the sudden turn of events and attitude my son demonstrated, I felt that perhaps the objections that he was sharing with me were legitimate and that I should check them out myself. I went to the school and shared the situation with administration and said that I intended to stand outside the classroom watching and listening to verify my son's complaints. He had NOT exaggerated one thing. The teacher was unfriendly, rolled her eyes, stomped her feet, huffed and puffed like the Big Bad Wolf that she was. This single event led to my son struggling when it came to elementary school. She single-handedly destroyed the joy of learning and attending school in the blink of an eye. Since that moment, we were able insure better teachers meeting certain personality requirements; however, we were never able to entirely reverse the damage that was done. Being a former kindergarten teacher, I was appalled by her behavior and by the school's lack of concern and/or effort to improve the situation for the students FORCED to attend school the remainder of the year. Unacceptable, ridiculous, and ABSOLUTELY true! Now, based upon this scenario, let it be known that sometimes students who appear unmotivated are simply damaged children who developed the attitude that they demonstrate along their educational path. However, some children have other issues with which they are dealing that can contribute to similar scenarios.

- As parents (and teachers) we need to make certain that the basic needs of our children are met BEFORE sending them to school. This includes a good night's rest, exercise during some portion of the day, a healthy diet including a substantial breakfast.

- As teachers, we should carefully examine the situation at hand and determine if there could be an underlying factor such as the child's inability to see the chalkboard clearly or to hear instruction(s). NOTE: Part of the reason for the difficulties my son experienced was a visual impairment that prevented him from focusing on letters, numbers, and symbols. For example, instead of seeing a + symbol, he saw two lines – one horizontal and one vertical. When he saw a lowercase letter "b" he actually saw a vertical line and a backwards letter "c" to the right. His teacher ASSUMED he was lazy when in fact he worked extremely hard but was incapable of overcoming his problem without medical attention.

- Make your classroom environment both stimulating and exciting. Nothing says "Ho Hum" like bare walls, a few bookshelves, and a calendar. Invite the students to join in decorating their environment and you'll see a sudden change in interest.

- Showing your children that you are earnestly interested in them as *people* is fundamental in building a relationship and the respect that you hope to encourage from your students.

- Plan your lessons carefully so that EVERY child can be successful on some level. Building self-esteem is vital to encouraging a child's interest and motivation.

- By implementing cooperative learning groups within your classroom you are taking the "dull" out of instruction and allowing the children to actively participate while engaging with others. This will encourage relationship building among the students and could, in fact, provide the unmotivated child with a motivation – to work alongside his friends.

- Help students establish realistic goals. Students that never meet goals lose interest, NOT because they're not interested, but because they are tired of feeling unsuccessful and often give up.

- Demonstrate enthusiasm when you teach. The teacher is the KEY to motivating students in the classroom, so "turn that frown upside down," teachers.

- Provide special recognition to each student throughout the day, week, month, and school year. By implementing "special" moments, children will feel enthusiastic and look forward to being "Student of the Month," "Line Leader for the Week," etc.

7. Students Lacking Respect:

- Some children will come into your classroom demonstrating an obvious lack of respect for you, his/her peers, other adults and their belongings, and/or the property of others. Teachers should practice and encourage the students to practice the Three R's (and I'm not talking about Reading, 'Riting, and 'Rithmatic") but instead Respect, Responsibility, and Reciprocity.

- Incorporating role-play in situations where there is an obvious lack of respect is a wonderful tool and can be used successfully at many age levels. For instance, when a child fails a test and is ridiculed and/or mocked by classmates, a wonderful "life lesson" would be for the teacher to immediately establish a group study identifying the situation that occurred and determining alternative actions that the students could have taken.

- Sometimes teaching children the Three R's is as simple as stating the reasons for respecting other people's property, other people, and being treated with respect in return. Publicly acknowledging a student's behavior when he/she demonstrates respectful behaviors is a great way of encouraging their peers to model their behavior in return.

- Make it clear to your students, through not just your words but your actions, that even though you are in charge of the class, you respect the individuals within your classroom and that you desire the same respect in return.

- Listen to your students. Never assume that you know what a student is going to say because more often than not, you'll be incorrect. Allow students to explain their actions. By establishing respect in allowing him or her to speak his/her mind (politely, of course) you have modeled respectful behavior and in turn will typically receive the same.

Effective behavior management in schools can be challenging and sometimes pose many difficult problems which we must overcome. Students come from a variety of backgrounds which often determine who they are without them even recognizing the impact, and they are then expected to function in an environment that often is contradictory to the environment(s) from which they've emerged. By establishing a welcoming and stimulating classroom environment, you can motivate students who appear to lack interest to become involved and participate alongside others. By creating a curriculum which allows for more movement and focuses on the interests of the students you'll engage even the most challenging students to focus and promote their success. By working along with your students you can teach them to be aware of "triggers" that lead them down the wrong path. Additionally, by helping them become familiar with emotions that are triggered in certain events, you can help them modify their behaviors into more appropriate and acceptable ones that will lend themselves better to a classroom environment.

In establishing a behavior management plan for your school and classroom, remember the following:

- Effective classroom instruction should include strategies that put into place school-wide procedures to reduce the development and occurrences of problem behavior by teaching and encouraging the appropriate behaviors among students and staff members.

- By establishing a welcoming environment which focuses on teaching and practicing the Three R's (Respect, Responsibility, and Reciprocity) you'll experience a more considerate group of students who will work together collectively to meet the established goals for themselves and others.

- By including instruction for intensive intervention within the classroom to address the particularly difficult behaviors and/or needs of your students by providing support, encouragement, and perhaps modified approaches to handling misbehavior, you'll be able to reach even the most distant of students and turn their negatives into positives. I've seen it happen many times and the rewards are outstanding.

This concludes Part VI of Positive Discipline, showing how important behavior management in schools can be obtained by implementing a solid plan encompassing strategies to help provide a proactive vs. reactive environment in which to teach. I hope you have learned many tips and strategies to help you with your children, grandchildren, nieces, nephews, and students. Parenting is hard work. No one ever said it was going to be easy – and if they did, well, they were obviously kidding. Hopefully, however, by utilizing the information that I have provided for you and your family, you will be able to reap the rewards of implementing more effective strategies in handling some of childhood's toughest challenges. Perhaps I've even saved you from going gray-headed prematurely.

Remember, first and foremost, we as adults must recognize that we have the most important responsibility as parents and teachers of children. We have the most rewarding opportunity to encourage the behaviors that we deem necessary for the successes of the wonderful creatures whose lives we've been blessed to touch and the most difficult job that we'll cherish forever.

Good luck, and remember, "Don't sweat the small stuff;" "Remember to praise the desired;" and, "Respect is a two-way street."